To Manda,
Good luck
Baking!

Chef Joycee

Cooking with *Jaxon*

Favorites from the Park City Cooking School

by Jaxon Stallard

Cooking with *Jaxon*

Favorites from the Park City Cooking School

Dedication

I take pleasure in dedicating this book to all the students, past, present, and future, who joined me in my kitchen or theirs. The questions they asked in their search for cooking and baking expertise and knowledge encouraged me to share my recipes, along with directions for successful results.

Every student, young and not so young, has been an inspiration to me. My thanks and warm regards to each and every one.

Jaxon S. Stallard, CCP

Published by Jaxon Stallard
6042 Fox Point Circle
Park City, Utah 84098

Food photography © by Steve Lalich
Hand shots by Roi Agnata
Portrait of Jaxon, biography page © AJF Photography

This cookbook is a collection of favorite recipes, which are not necessarily original recipes.

Library of Congress Control Number: 2008902872
ISBN: 978-1-60402-954-3

Edited, Designed, and Manufactured by
Favorite Recipes® Press
An imprint of

FRP.

P.O. Box 305142
Nashville, Tennessee 37230
800-358-0560

Art Direction and Book Design: Steve Newman
Project Editor: Nicki Pendleton Wood

Manufactured in the United States of America
First Printing: 2008
6,000 copies

Acknowledgments

Special thanks to my daughters—Jacqueline, Charlene, Rondi, and Alison—and my son, Elgin, for their support and love all along the way. They have given me inspiration and a special purpose to my life.

From the beginning, there have been many creative people who helped and supported me along my culinary journey.

To Susie Schultz, Julie Monahan, Joanne Kaeske, Patti Johnson, Norma Mitchell, Mehl Cimini, and Julie Joyce, all accomplished cooks before they ever came to my kitchen, a special thank-you for sharing your expertise when I really needed it. To Roi Agnata, thanks to you for the outstanding "how-to" photos. Somehow, Roi always made my hands look younger than the years of kneading and rolling dough would imply.

To the Mountain Munchers—Reg and Sadonna Leeby, Dick and Sue Worley, Roi and Joan Agnata, Mehl and Gloria Cimini, and Kerry Kelly—thanks for inviting me into your kitchens to have the time of my life and for your constant inspiration to finish this cookbook.

A warm thanks to those at FRP who coached me when I had no idea where to turn next, specifically Bill Branch, Mary Cummings, and Julee Hicks for coaching me on design and other major decisions on the "look" of the finished product.

And thank you to all my friends and students who from start to finish wanted to see this cookbook project succeed. Oftentimes they put aside their own work to help me with testing, proofing, and offering suggestions that have contributed significantly. Thanks to Mary Ann Vennett for putting my words in order so eloquently. Somehow along this journey my friend and student, Jane Bauer, agreed to contribute her expertise in wine pairings. I owe special thanks to her for writing about wine the way I love to write about food.

And finally, warm appreciation and gratitude to Steve and Susan Lalich and Julee Rauch of Lalich Resources and to food stylist Susan Massey for sharing their talents and skills and offering their support.

*F*rom her formative years in west Texas to her current home in the Wasatch Mountains of Utah, Jaxon Stallard's academic, personal, and professional careers took her on an odyssey across the United States from San Francisco to Boston and points in between, culminating in an international posting in Doha, Qatar, where as dental professionals she and her late husband, Dr. Richard E. Stallard, established and operated a multidiscipline dental clinic for twenty years.

Cooking has always been important to Jaxon, and this expatriate experience coupled with world travel provided exposure to various indigenous cuisines and nourished her interest in the culinary arts. During that tenure, she wrote a cookbook for the American Women of Qatar, introducing local cuisine and incorporating readily available ingredients into existing American recipes.

When Jaxon returned to the States in 1997 she made the decision to pursue her burgeoning passion—cooking, baking, and teaching the joys of both. After graduating from the Cambridge School of Culinary Arts in 1999 and completing an apprenticeship in the Netherlands, Jaxon relocated to California where in addition to teaching professional cooking classes she opened a full-service bakery in the city of San Luis Obispo.

Biography

Since moving to Park City, Utah, in 2002 this mother of five, grandmother of six, and great-grandmother of one has launched the Park City Cooking School, bringing to fruition her aspired vocation as a professional chef and culinary arts instructor. Today, Jaxon shares her development of recipes, preferences for ingredients, cooking techniques, and "intense desire to eat delicious food" by offering year-round interactive classes and workshops for adults and hands-on Kids Cooking Classes for the young.

In 2005 Jaxon achieved the distinction of Certified Culinary Professional from the International Association of Culinary Professionals.

Mary Ann Vennett

JAXON

I love food . . . Most of my life is spent cooking, baking, talking, and writing about food, and I spend most of that time in my kitchen developing recipes.

With that in mind, I like to know where the food I use comes from. When I can't grow my own vegetables, I try to get them at a farmers' market or from local growers that offer wonderful options for high-quality, locally grown and raised foods. Whenever possible, I buy regionally produced eggs and dairy products. They are always fresher and taste amazingly better than those traveling long distances from questionable sources. And why would I buy lamb from New Zealand when the best is raised right here in Utah? I am sure that wherever you live, there is a source nearby that offers fresh produce, meat, and dairy products, including artisanal cheese.

Notes from Jaxon

Although I love to spend time in my kitchen, I try to make food preparation easier by challenging myself to simplify cooking and baking by spending less time in the kitchen and still being able to produce delicious results. Many people think they don't have the time, or they don't realize how quickly they can prepare a delectable, homecooked meal. In this book, as well as in my classes, I strive to offer realistic ways to prepare meals that beckon friends and family to return to the days of sitting together around the table at home having dinner.

When I started selecting and organizing my recipes for this book, I had no clear vision of what the final product would be. The first step was to take a closer look at all my students' favorite recipes, from the first professional cooking classes I taught at the bakery to my current classes at the Park City Cooking School. This led to a series of "the next step was," resulting in *Cooking with Jaxon*, which offers a collection of select, best-liked recipes waiting to be prepared and served by you.

Table of Contents

All the recipes in this book were formulated and tested at high altitude.

Before You Begin

Mise en place (MEEZ ahn plahs)

A French term referring to assembling beforehand all the ingredients necessary for a dish. To organize efficiently, use appropriate size glass, plastic, or metal bowls to hold measured ingredients. I go so far as to prepare the pan or pot that will be used to cook or bake in as well as the serving or holding dishes.

The attention of setting out and measuring ingredients helps you focus on the task at hand. You will be less likely forget an ingredient or measure incorrectly. Mise en place promotes pleasure in both baking and cooking and more successful results.

Measuring

In a very few recipes, inaccurate measurements of a certain ingredient may not spoil the dish. Examples include raisins, nuts, chocolate chips, coconut, or even vanilla. However, for tender cakes with a perfect crumb, you must measure the baking soda, baking powder, salt, cocoa powder, and flour carefully. Even in the simplest recipes, baking is not as forgiving as other cooking.

Flour   When a recipe calls for 1 cup all-purpose flour, this means measure before sifting (if the recipe calls for sifting). When the flour sits in a canister, it can settle. It is a good idea to stir the flour before measuring. Spoon the flour lightly into a dry measure until it is overfilled. Run a flat-edge spatula or knife across the rim to level the flour.

If a recipe calls for 1 cup sifted flour, the flour should be sifted before measuring. Again, you need to overfill the cup, and then run a flat-edge spatula or knife across the rim of the cup to level the flour.

Unsweetened baking cocoa   Normally recipes call for unsifted cocoa. However, if your cocoa is very lumpy and compacted, press out most of the lumps with the back of a spoon, then stir it a little to loosen before measuring it like unsifted flour (see above).

Measuring tools

Dry measures are designed to measure dry ingredients and are usually available in $1/4$, $1/3$, $1/2$, and 1 cup sizes. Unless the recipe calls for a packed or lightly packed cup, heap dry ingredients above the rim of the cup as described for flour. Run a flat-edge spatula or a knife across the top to level it. For dry measures, I prefer steel to plastic in both measuring cups and spoons.

Liquid measures are clear glass or plastic containers designed to measure liquids; they usually have pouring spouts and lines up the sides to indicate measurements. Be sure to set the measure on the countertop before pouring in the liquid. You will be able to see the accurate level.

I have 1-cup, 2-cup, 4-cup, and 8-cup glass measures with small increments on the sides.

You will need $1/8$, $1/4$, $1/2$, 1 teaspoon, and 1 tablespoon size spoon measures. Avoid buying any "off" measure spoons or cups—it is too easy to grab the wrong size.

I also have several shotglass-size measures with increments on the sides to help the Kids in the Kitchen measure very small amounts of liquid. It's easier than fumbling with spoons.

Mixing

For better results, use the type of mixing utensil suggested in each recipe. Mixing with a wooden spoon does not give the same texture and results as a spoon-shaped silicone spatula. When a recipe calls for mixing, folding, or stirring "just until the ingredient is incorporated," this means that extra mixing may deflate the batter, resulting in a tough cake or cookie or other problems.

Tools and equipment

Baking parchment   I use baking parchment to line half-sheet pans when baking cookies or sheet cakes and for lining cake pan bottoms, to name just a few uses.

Baking sheet pans   Professional aluminum half-sheet pans, which measure 12 × 17-inches, fit most home ovens and perform much better than lighter weight 11 × 17-inch home kitchen jelly roll pans. You can buy them at specialty cookware stores, restaurant supply stores, and warehouse grocery discount stores.

Bowls   Stainless steel and glass mixing bowls are used for different purposes. Glass bowls are good for melting chocolate or butter in the microwave. Stainless steel bowls are good for using as the top of a double boiler. Deep bowls are best for beating egg whites and whipping cream. One- or two-quart glass measures with handles also make wonderful mixing bowls and are good for melting chocolate in the microwave.

Cake pan   You can get good results from light-colored, heavy-duty pans without breaking the bank. Lightweight cake pans are not recommended, as they warp in the oven. I prefer cake pans with 2-inch sides, but I do have an abundance of 3-inch pans that work for me. Cheesecake pans should always have a removable bottom for ease of removal. If you use removable bottom pans, you will need to wrap the bottom with heavy-duty foil if baking the cheesecake in a water bath (bain-marie).

Cooling Racks   Racks for cooling cakes and cookies speed up the cooling process and keep baked goods from getting soggy. I have in my kitchen a commercial "speed rack" that holds thirty half-sheet pans for cooling (and serves as storage as well). For the home kitchen, there are multi-tiered racks that hold either four half-sheet pans or cooling racks. The racks fold away when not needed.

Food processors   The processor is invaluable for mixing certain bread doughs as well as mixing up pasta dough. It can be used for other tasks as well. I nearly always avoid them for chopping nuts. I prefer the clean cut of a sharp chef knife on the edges of nuts. To make superfine sugar, simply measure the amount of sugar needed into the bowl of the food processor fitted with the metal blade and process for about 30 seconds.

Microwave oven   I use the microwave for heating liquids, melting butter and chocolate, and a few other tasks.

Mixers I use a KitchenAid stand mixer for mixing batters, bread doughs, and pasta (using its special pasta attachment). Another use for the pasta roller is rolling out the Wine and Black Pepper Cracker Bread (page 37).

Pastry Bag and Tips Disposable pastry bags are inexpensive and easily accessible to the modern home cook. If you are garnishing dishes or decorating cakes and cookies, I would recommend having some on hand. If you have pastry bags, then you need a small assortment of tips, from 1/8 to 3/4 inch and several star tips.

Rolling Pin The choice of a rolling pin is a subjective one. I have an assortment of sizes, diameters, and materials. My favorite is a heavy wooden pin with bearings for ease with the handles. My next favorite is a long silicone one with handles and a small diameter. None is better than the others—choose the one that best suits your needs.

Spatulas The new silicone spatulas are great for cooking everything from custards to caramel. They come in several sizes, with the largest being used for folding meringue into delicate batters and scraping large bowls.

Strainers A large fine-mesh strainer does the job for flour and other dry ingredients. It requires only one hand and it shakes out clean after each use. I like a medium-size strainer for removing the bits (called chalaze) from cooked custards. Small fine-mesh strainers are best for dusting desserts with confectioners' sugar or cocoa.

Thermometers I like the combination timer/thermometer made by several manufacturers. It has a probe attached to a wire that can be inserted into a pot of candy on top of the stove, meat, or a loaf of bread in the oven.

Wire whisks An essential hand tool and not just for beating. Whisks are better than kitchen forks for mixing dry ingredients or fluffing up flour before it is added to a batter.

Zester microplane Lifts off a thin shred of zest without any bitter white pith. A must in the kitchen. Grates hard cheeses nicely, too.

Ingredients

Baking powder and baking soda Cakes may be leavened with either baking powder or baking soda. Baking powder has an expiration period and will lose its leavening power if not fresh. It should be stored in an airtight container and not used beyond its expiration date.

Butter I have tried most brands available in the United States and some in Europe. It was by chance that I discovered the best all-around butter, in my opinion: Unsalted Mid-America Butter, sold at Sam's Club. Margarine is not usually a good substitute in my recipes. I also don't usually use shortening. However, I do use the new 0 grams Trans Fat Crisco for a couple of recipes.

Cream The cleanest-tasting cream is simply pasteurized rather than ultra-pasteurized and contains no added ingredients. I like to purchase cream packaged without the stabilizer carrageenan, even though it does produce smoother whipped cream.

Eggs   The fresher the better. Use Grade AA large eggs for the recipes in this book. If possible, buy free-range eggs from a reputable farmer. Keep them in the coldest part of the refrigerator and never leave them out for any reason other than to come to room temperature for baking and cooking.

Extracts   Use pure extracts if at all possible.

Flour   For the sake of continuity and predictability, find a brand of flour you like and stick with it. The recipes in this book were developed and tested with unbleached all-purpose or bread flour.

Nuts   Choose fresh nuts that are raw, not toasted, and offered in bulk from stores with a big turnover, rather than packaged nuts from the supermarket. Larger halves and pieces stay fresh longer; chop them yourself. I keep nuts in the freezer in airtight packages. Toast nuts before cooking or baking with them to bring out their rich flavor and crunchy texture. Cool before chopping.

Spices   Purchase spices in small quantities, and in whole form when possible (cloves, allspice, nutmeg, and peppercorns, for instance). Before using, toast spice in a dry sauté pan and grind in a spice grinder or coffee grinder reserved for spices. Store in a dry, airtight container.

Sugar   I like cane sugar best. Superfine sugar is better for meringues and caramels of all kinds.

Vanilla   Always use only pure vanilla extract. Bourbon vanilla from Madagascar and Mexican vanilla are my choices. Vanilla bean paste is another good option.

Mixing ingredients

Add and mix ingredients in the order called for in the steps. This can be critical.

Many recipes call for whisking the flour and other dry ingredients in order to blend them into batters without excessive mixing.

Very delicate cakes, such as sponge or génoise, call for dry ingredients to be sifted two or three times. This aerates the dry ingredients so they blend easily into the batter with minimal mixing.

Tender baked goods are often a matter of proper measuring, mixing, and timing. Using the wrong kind of flour and overmixing will almost always result in a tough product. Baking too long or at a temperature that is too high or too low also causes tough cakes, cookies, and pastries.

Ingredient temperature

When the recipe calls for butter, milk, eggs, meat, fish, or any usually refrigerated ingredient to be at room temperature, that usually means around 65 to 75 degrees. The ingredient should still be slightly cool.

Quick ways to bring some ingredients to room temperature:

- Put cracked eggs in a stainless steel or glass bowl set in a larger bowl of warm water and whisk gently until blended; let stand until no longer cold.
- Microwave milk or other liquids for just a few seconds, or set the measuring cup in a bowl of hot water just until no longer cold.
- Cut butter into chunks and microwave on Low for a few seconds at a time until pliable but not melted.

Creative Beginings

Gravlax—The Simple Way

Makes 18 to 24 servings

1 (3- to 4-pound) salmon fillet
2 tablespoons bourbon or vodka
1/3 cup kosher salt or sea salt
2 tablespoons light brown sugar
1 teaspoon crushed allspice
1/2 teaspoon crushed black peppercorns
1/2 teaspoon crushed white peppercorn

Gravlax is a Swedish specialty of salt-cured salmon. Reserve any unused cure mixture for another time.

1 Remove the pin bones from the salmon fillet with needlenose pliers, taking care not to bruise the fish. Cut the fillet into equal halves. Sprinkle both halves with the bourbon.

2 Mix the salt, brown sugar, allspice and peppercorns together. Place one portion of the fillet skin side down on a work surface. Press a generous amount of the salt mixture into the fillet. Place the remaining portion of the fillet skin side up on the top.

3 Moisten a piece of cheesecloth and squeeze it dry. Place the fish on the cheesecloth and wrap tightly. Place on an 18×18-inch piece of plastic wrap and wrap tightly. Place in a glass or ceramic dish with sides 2 to 4 inches deep. Place a second empty dish on top of the salmon and weight with as many filled cans or bottles as possible.

4 Cure in the refrigerator for 2 days, turning the fish over every 12 hours. Remove the weights, cheesecloth and plastic wrap and discard any liquid that has formed during the curing process. Rewrap with plastic wrap and continue to cure for 2 days longer. The texture should be dry, and the fat should glisten on the surface, preventing a knife from sticking to the flesh.

5 Slice the fillet as thinly as possible on a low diagonal to create the largest slices possible. Serve plain, with Gravlax Sauce or with a dressing of your choice.

Gravlax Sauce

Makes 1 1/2 cups

1 cup heavy cream, or 1/2 cup sour cream
    and 1/2 cup light cream
1/4 cup sweet yellow mustard, or to taste
Sugar, salt and freshly cracked pepper to taste
Bourbon or other spirit of choice to taste
1 tablespoon minced fresh chives

Special kitchen equipment
needlenose pliers; cheesecloth

Mix the cream with the mustard in a small bowl. Season with sugar, salt, pepper and bourbon. Chill, covered, for 2 hours or longer. Stir in the chives at serving time.

Scallops on Asian Risotto Cakes with Cilantro Pesto

Cilantro Pesto

1 Combine the peanuts, cilantro, garlic, ginger and white pepper in a blender or food processor. Process until minced. Add the lime juice, sugar, fish sauce and peanut oil gradually, processing constantly until smooth. Spoon into a serving dish. Set aside.

Asian Risotto Cakes

2 Combine the stock, mirin, fish sauce, water, lemon grass, lime leaves and cilantro in a saucepan. Bring to a boil and maintain at a simmer.

3 Heat the butter and 1 tablespoon peanut oil in a large saucepan over medium heat until bubbling. Add the shallots, scallions, garlic, ginger and white pepper. Cook for 2 to 3 minutes or until the shallots and scallions are tender and the ginger is fragrant. Add the rice and stir to coat well.

4 Remove the lemon grass, lime leaves and cilantro sprigs from the stock mixture. Stir 1/2 cup of the stock into the rice. Cook over medium heat until nearly all of the liquid is absorbed. Add the remaining stock 1/2 cup at a time and cook for 20 to 25 minutes after each addition or until the stock is absorbed, cooking until the rice is tender and stirring constantly.

5 Spread the rice on a large baking sheet and cool to room temperature. Chill, covered with plastic wrap, for 3 hours. Divide the risotto into four balls and press into patties. Wrap with plastic wrap and chill for 10 minutes longer.

6 Heat 2 tablespoons peanut oil in a large sauté pan over medium heat. Dust the risotto patties with the flour and sauté in batches in the oil for 2 minutes on each side or until crisp. Drain on paper towels and cover loosely with foil to keep warm.

Scallops

7 Heat a small amount of canola oil in a skillet over high heat. Dry the scallops with a paper towel and add to the skillet in batches. Sear for 1 minute on each side or until golden brown. Place one Asian Risotto Cake in the center of each serving plate. Arrange three scallops on each cake and top with Cilantro Pesto. Garnish with lime wedges.

Makes 4 servings

Cilantro Pesto
2 tablespoons chopped
*   unsalted peanuts*
1 cup cilantro, minced
2 garlic cloves, minced
1 teaspoon minced fresh ginger
1/4 teaspoon white pepper
1/4 cup fresh lime juice
1 to 2 teaspoons sugar
1 tablespoon fish sauce
1 tablespoon (or more) peanut oil

Asian Risotto Cakes
2 cups vegetable stock
2 tablespoons mirin (rice wine)
1 tablespoon fish sauce
1 cup water
1 stalk lemon grass,
*   white portions only, bruised*
2 kaffir lime leaves
3 sprigs cilantro
3/4 ounce Clarified Butter (page 117)
1 tablespoon peanut oil
3 red Asian shallots, thinly sliced
4 scallions, chopped
3 garlic cloves, chopped
2 tablespoons finely chopped
*   fresh ginger*
1 teaspoon white pepper
2/3 cup uncooked arborio rice
2 tablespoons peanut oil
1/4 cup all-purpose flour

Scallops
Canola oil for sautéing
12 large scallops
Lime wedges, for garnish

Special kitchen equipment
blender or food processor

Marinated Shrimp with Champagne Beurre Blanc

Makes 8 servings

1 cup Champagne or other dry
    sparkling wine
1/4 cup extra-virgin olive oil
3 tablespoons minced shallots
1/2 teaspoon freshly ground pepper
24 large uncooked shrimp, peeled with tails
    intact and deveined (about 2 pounds)
Champagne Beurre Blanc (below)
1 tablespoon minced fresh chives
1 tablespoon fresh tarragon
1 tablespoon minced fresh parsley

1 Combine the Champagne, olive oil, shallots and pepper in a resealable plastic bag. Add the shrimp and seal the bag. Shake to coat the shrimp evenly. Marinate at room temperature for 30 to 60 minutes, turning the bag occasionally.

2 Spray a broiler pan with nonstick cooking spray. Drain the shrimp, discarding the marinade. Arrange the shrimp in a single layer in the prepared pan. Broil in a preheated broiler for 2 minutes on each side or just until opaque in the centers.

3 Stand three shrimp with tails upright in the centers of eight serving plates. Spoon warm Champagne Beurre Blanc around the shrimp. Sprinkle with the chives, tarragon and parsley.

Champagne Beurre Blanc

Makes about 1 1/2 cups

2 cups Champagne
1/3 cup finely chopped shallots
2 tablespoons Champagne vinegar
1/4 teaspoon black peppercorns
1 cup (2 sticks) unsalted butter, chilled and
    cut into 16 pieces
Salt and pepper to taste

The Champagne gives this classic, and amazingly easy, French butter sauce a glamorous makeover, but you can also use a less expensive dry sparkling wine.

1 Combine the Champagne, shallots, vinegar and peppercorns in a heavy medium saucepan. Bring to a boil and cook for 20 minutes or until reduced to 1/4 cup. This can be prepared in advance, covered, and allowed to stand at room temperature for up to 4 hours.

2 Reheat the Champagne mixture over medium-low heat if it has been allowed to cool. Whisk in the butter one piece at a time, allowing each to just melt before adding another; do not allow the sauce to boil. Season with salt and pepper.

Artichoke and White Bean Spread

Topping

1 Toss the artichokes lightly with the flour. Heat the canola oil in a large sauté pan. Add the artichokes and sauté until crisp. Remove to paper towels to drain.

Spread

2 Heat 2 tablespoons olive oil in a medium sauté pan over medium-high heat until it begins to shimmer. Add the artichokes and sauté for 2 to 3 minutes. Reduce the heat to medium and add the shallots and thyme. Sauté until the shallots are tender. Add the beans and sauté for 2 to 4 minutes longer.

3 Spoon the mixture into a blender and add the cheese, Roasted Garlic and lemon juice; process until smooth. Strain through a fine-mesh strainer or press through a food mill to remove any bean skins or hard pieces of artichoke.

Presentation

4 Brush the baguette slices with the olive oil and arrange on a serving plate. Top each slice with several arugula leaves. Spread with a spoonful of the spread and top with additional arugula leaves and the artichoke topping. Drizzle with Balsamic Reduction. Season with salt and pepper. Serve within the hour.

Variation: This is a good way to enjoy artichokes when they are not in season. When they are in season and abundant, you can substitute ten fresh artichokes for the frozen artichokes. Remove the firm outer leaves and cores and submerge the artichokes in a bowl of water mixed with the juice of one lemon. Drain and air-dry the artichokes. Use six of the artichokes in the spread. Chop the remaining four artichokes into 1/4-inch pieces and use them in the topping.

Makes 3 cups

Artichoke Topping
16 frozen artichoke quarters,
*   thawed, drained and chopped*
1 cup all-purpose flour
1 cup canola oil

Spread
2 tablespoons olive oil
8 frozen artichoke quarters,
*   thawed and drained*
1 tablespoon minced shallots
1 tablespoon minced fresh thyme
1 1/2 cups cooked white cannellini
*   beans or navy beans*
2 ounces goat cheese,
*   at room temperature*
Roasted Garlic (page 114)
Juice of 1 lemon

Presentation
8 to 10 thin slices
*   (or more) baguette*
2 tablespoons olive oil
Arugula leaves
Balsamic Reduction (page 116)
Salt and pepper to taste

Special kitchen equipment
blender; fine-mesh strainer or
*   food mill*

Avocado Mousse

Makes 1¹/2 cups

2 ripe avocados, sliced
(Hass avocados are recommended)
1 tablespoon lemon juice
1¹/2 teaspoons fresh thyme
1 teaspoon salt
¹/4 teaspoon freshly ground white pepper
¹/2 cup crème fraîche or sour cream

Special kitchen equipment
food processor; 12-inch pastry bag fitted
with a 1-inch star tip (optional)

1 Combine the avocados, lemon juice, thyme, salt and white pepper in a food processor; pulse until smooth. Remove to a small bowl and fold in the crème fraîche. Chill, covered with plastic wrap, for 1 to 12 hours.

2 Spoon into a pastry bag fitted with a 1-inch star tip if desired. Pipe as desired or serve as suggested below.

Note: A silky avocado mousse is one of those rare restaurant recipes that is easy to make at home. It is a great topper for baked potatoes, steak, roast, fish, burgers, or grilled corn, but that is only the beginning! Other applications include dipping sauce for crudités or grilled shrimp; filling for cherry tomato hors d'oeuvre; topping for swordfish kabobs; spread for turkey club sandwiches, bagels and lox; or crab quesadillas.

Baba Ghanoush (Eggplant Dip)

Makes 1 to 1¹/2 cups

1 large eggplant, stem end trimmed
¹/3 cup lemon juice
¹/3 cup sesame oil
1 large garlic clove, roasted (optional)
¹/2 teaspoon kosher salt
Minced parsley, for garnish
Pomegranate seeds, for garnish
Olive oil for drizzling

Special kitchen equipment
food processor (optional)

1 Place the eggplant on a baking sheet. Bake at 400 degrees for 1 hour or until very tender and collapsed onto the baking sheet. Let stand until cool to the touch. Scoop the pulp from the skin and purée in a food processor or mash in a bowl.

2 Add the lemon juice gradually, alternating with the sesame oil and processing or stirring constantly. Season with the garlic and kosher salt, beating until nearly smooth. Spoon into a serving bowl and garnish with minced parsley and rows of pomegranate seeds. Drizzle with olive oil. Serve with scallions, radishes and toasted pita wedges.

Note: When I lived in the Middle East, I found that baba ghanoush and hummus were favorite appetizer/dips and were served at most events. Baba ghanoush is best served at room temperature; traditionally, pita bread is used as a scoop for the dip.

Caponata of Smoky Vegetables

1 Arrange the tomatoes on a baking sheet. Roast at 400 degrees for 20 to 30 minutes. Cool to room temperature and cut into 1/2-inch pieces.

2 Combine the eggplant, squash, onion and bell peppers in a large bowl. Add 2 tablespoons olive oil, 1 teaspoon salt and 1/2 teaspoon pepper; toss to coat evenly. Grill on a preheated grill for 1 minute on each side or until marked by the grill. Remove with tongs and cool to room temperature. Chop into 1/2-inch pieces.

3 Heat 1 tablespoon olive oil in a large heavy saucepan over high heat. Add the eggplant mixture and sauté for 1 minute. Add the garlic, 1 teaspoon salt and 1 teaspoon pepper. Sauté until the vegetables are tender but hold their shape.

4 Remove from the heat and stir in 1/4 cup extra-virgin olive oil, the balsamic vinegar, sherry vinegar, pine nuts, capers, basil and parsley. Cool to room temperature. Add the roasted tomatoes and mix well. Chill, covered, for 6 hours or longer to develop the flavor.

Makes 8 cups

2 ripe tomatoes, cut into quarters
1 small eggplant, sliced
   3/4 inch thick
1 large yellow squash,
   sliced 1/2 inch thick
1 small red onion, sliced
   1/2 inch thick
1 red bell pepper, cut into halves
1 yellow bell pepper, cut into halves
2 tablespoons olive oil
1 teaspoon salt
1/2 teaspoon freshly ground pepper
1 tablespoon olive oil
2 tablespoons minced garlic
1 teaspoon salt
1 teaspoon freshly ground pepper
1/4 cup extra-virgin olive oil
1/4 cup balsamic vinegar
1/4 cup sherry vinegar
1/4 cup pine nuts, lightly toasted
2 tablespoons capers, drained
2 tablespoons minced fresh basil
2 tablespoons minced fresh parsley

Serve this Sicilian specialty plain, as a sauce for pasta, as a dip with toasted pita bread wedges, or, my favorite, as a sandwich filling. The flavor is best when it is served at room temperature.

Special kitchen equipment
*outdoor grill or indoor electric
   grill; tongs*

1 cup dried chickpeas
1 rib celery, minced
1 carrot, minced
1/2 small onion, minced
1 red bell pepper
1 cup water
1/2 cup couscous
1/2 cup minced flat-leaf parsley
1/2 cup minced fresh oregano
1/4 cup olive oil
Salt and freshly ground pepper to taste
Roasted Garlic Sauce (page 21)
3/4 cup crumbled feta cheese

$\mathcal{M}$ost feta cheese is made from sheep's milk, but it can also be made with goat's milk or cow's milk; very good feta is now made in the United States. It is not a complex cheese, but when correctly made, it crumbles evenly as it slices. Look for a cheese that is creamy with just the right salt content.

Special kitchen equipment
cheesecloth; food processor;
    six decorative serving spoons (optional)

Chickpeas with Feta Cheese and Roasted Garlic Sauce

1 Combine the chickpeas with enough water to cover by several inches in a large bowl. Let stand for 6 to 12 hours. Drain and place in a large stockpot. Add enough water to cover by 3 inches.

2 Tie the celery, carrot and onion in a 10-inch square of cheesecloth. Add to the stockpot and bring to a boil. Boil for 3 to 5 minutes, skimming any foam that rises to the surface. Reduce the heat and simmer for 45 to 60 minutes or until the chickpeas are tender and cooked through; add additional water as needed to keep the chickpeas covered.

3 Drain, discarding the cheesecloth packet. Place the chickpeas in a large bowl and cool to room temperature. Chill, covered, in the refrigerator.

4 Place the bell pepper on a rack in a broiler pan and place in a preheated broiler. Broil for 10 to 15 minutes or until the pepper is tender and the skin is blistered and charred. (You can also place the pepper on a long fork and char it over a gas flame.) Place the pepper in a small bowl. Cover with plastic wrap and steam for 10 minutes. Rub the charred skin from the pepper and chop the pepper into 1/2-inch pieces, discarding the seeds and membranes.

5 Bring 1 cup water to a boil in a medium saucepan and stir in the couscous. Remove from the heat and cover tightly; let stand for 5 minutes. Fluff the couscous with a fork and spoon into a medium bowl. Chill, covered, in the refrigerator.

6 Add the couscous to the chickpeas. Add the roasted bell pepper, parsley, oregano and olive oil. Season with salt and pepper. Spread the Roasted Garlic Sauce in a bowl and top with the chickpea mixture and cheese. You can also process the chickpea mixture in a food processor and serve by spreading the Roasted Garlic Sauce in the bowls of six to eight decorative serving spoons. Top each with about 1/4 cup of the chickpea mixture. Sprinkle the tops with the cheese.

Roasted Garlic Sauce

Makes about 1/2 cup

2 garlic bulbs
Olive oil
Salt and pepper to taste

1 Slice off the tops of the garlic bulbs and brush the tops of the exposed garlic cloves evenly with olive oil. Wrap each bulb in foil and place in a small baking pan. Roast in a preheated 300-degree oven for 30 minutes or until very tender. Cool to room temperature. Store in the refrigerator until needed.

2 Squeeze the bottoms of the garlic bulbs to remove the roasted cloves from the skins; discard the skins. Mash the pulp with a wooden spoon in a small bowl, adding enough olive oil to make a sauce-like consistency. Season with salt and pepper. Chill, covered, until serving time.

Champagne or other dry sparkling wines pair well with starters and appetizers, as they bring a festive feeling to the beginning of your meal or party. The bubbles from the wine cleanse the palate and complement the flavors in recipes designed to tease the appetite.

Brie en Croûte

Makes 10 to 12 servings

2 tablespoons Clarified Butter (page 117)
1 pear, peeled and cut into 1/2-inch pieces
1/4 cup pear brandy
1 tablespoon brown sugar
1 (7- or 8-inch) wheel Brie cheese
2 (12×18-inch) sheets frozen puff pastry,
    thawed and chilled, or Classic Puff Pastry
    (page 118)
2 eggs
Pinch of sugar

I like to use different fillings for the Brie, depending on the season and the fresh fruits available. Fresh fig preserves and Cranberry Fruit Compote (page 121) are two of my favorites.

Special kitchen equipment
baking parchment; small pastry brush

1 Heat the butter in a medium sauté pan over medium-high heat. Add the pear and sauté until almost tender. Add the pear brandy and stir to deglaze the sauté pan. Cook until the liquid is almost completely reduced. Reduce the heat to medium-low. Add the brown sugar and cook until the pear is caramelized. Cool completely.

2 Cut the cheese wheel into halves horizontally with a warm, dry sharp knife. Spread the caramelized pear over the bottom half and place the top half of the wheel over the pear; press lightly. Chill for 15 minutes.

3 Roll one sheet of the puff pastry larger that the cheese wheel on a work surface. Place the cheese container on the pastry and press down lightly to make a slight indentation. Cut a circle 4 inches larger than the container for the top crust. Repeat the process, cutting the second circle the exact size of the cheese container for the bottom crust. Chill the pastry circles.

4 Whisk the eggs with the sugar in a small bowl. Strain into a clear glass bowl. Place the larger pastry circle on a sheet of baking parchment on a work surface. Brush the egg over the surface of the pastry with a pastry brush, taking care not to allow the egg to drip over the edge, as it will cause the pastry to stick to the baking parchment.

6 Place the chilled cheese wheel in the center of the pastry and top with the smaller circle. Lift the edge of the lower pastry up over the upper pastry, pleating to fit and pressing gently to secure the edges. Invert the wheel and brush the top and side of the pastry with the remaining egg.

7 Place on a baking parchment-lined rimless baking sheet. Bake in a preheated 410-degree oven for 20 minutes. Reduce the oven temperature to 350 degrees and bake until the pastry is golden brown. Let stand at room temperature for 10 minutes. Place on a serving platter and serve with crackers arranged around the edge of the platter.

Blue Cheese and Bacon Puffs

Makes 5 dozen 2-inch puffs

3 thick slices bacon, chopped
1 cup vegetable stock or chicken stock
6 tablespoons unsalted butter, softened
1/2 teaspoon kosher salt
1/4 teaspoon freshly ground white pepper
1/4 teaspoon cayenne pepper
1 cup all-purpose flour
4 eggs
2/3 cup crumbled blue cheese
1/4 cup grated Parmesan cheese
1/4 cup thinly sliced scallions

These puffs are great with cocktails, but they make a good accompaniment to salads as well. The tops can be cut off and the puffs filled with lobster mousse for an extra-special event. They have the added appeal that they can be baked in advance and frozen for up to 1 month. Allow them to thaw at room temperature and reheat at 400 degrees on a baking sheet lined with baking parchment to serve.

Special kitchen equipment
stand mixer fitted with a paddle attachment;
small spring-action ice cream scoop;
baking parchment

1 Sauté the bacon in a small skillet over medium-high heat until crisp. Drain on paper towels.

2 Combine the stock, butter, kosher salt, white pepper and cayenne pepper in a medium saucepan. Bring to a boil over medium heat. Add the flour all at once and stir with a wooden spoon until the mixture forms a ball around the spoon. Cook until the mixture begins to stick to the bottom and side of the saucepan. Cool slightly.

3 Place the dough in a stand mixer fitted with a paddle. Beat in the eggs one at a time at medium speed. Stir in the cheeses, scallions and bacon.

4 Scoop the dough with a spoon or small ice cream scoop 2 inches apart onto a baking parchment-lined baking sheet. Place on a rack in the lower third of a preheated 300-degree oven. Increase the oven temperature to 400 degrees. Bake for 20 to 25 minutes or until puffed and brown. Turn off the oven and let the puffs stand in the oven until crisp and deep golden brown. Serve warm or at room temperature.

Blue Cheese-Stuffed Portobello Mushrooms

1 Wipe the caps of the mushrooms with a dampened paper towel and remove the stems. Scrape the gills gently from the caps with a grapefruit spoon.

2 Heat 2 tablespoons olive oil in a large skillet until moderately hot. Add the onion and cook for 15 minutes or until tender and light brown. Add the garlic, thyme, salt and pepper. Cook for 5 to 7 minutes longer. Stir in the wine and cook for 10 minutes or until the liquid is reduced by two-thirds. Add the spinach and cook until the spinach is wilted. Spoon into a bowl.

3 Wipe the skillet and pour in 2 tablespoons olive oil. Place the mushrooms stem side up in the skillet and cook over medium heat for 2 minutes. Turn the mushrooms over and cook for 2 minutes longer. Season with salt and pepper.

4 Turn the mushrooms over again and spoon the spinach mixture into the caps; spoon the pan juices over the mushrooms. Add the water to the skillet and simmer for 5 minutes or until the mushrooms are tender. Crumble the cheese over the tops and cover the skillet. Simmer for 2 minutes or until the cheese melts. Serve on a plate lined with salad greens.

Makes 4 servings

4 medium or 10 small
    portobello mushrooms
2 tablespoons olive oil
1 large yellow onion, thinly sliced
3 garlic cloves, minced
1 tablespoon minced fresh thyme
Salt and freshly ground pepper
    to taste
1 cup port
4 cups loosely packed spinach,
    coarsely chopped
2 tablespoons olive oil
1 tablespoon water
2 ounces blue cheese
6 ounces salad greens

For a starter or main-course salad, toss fresh spinach with a small amount of olive oil and balsamic vinegar, top with the portobello mushrooms and pour the hot pan juices over the top to wilt the spinach.

Special kitchen equipment
grapefruit spoon with a serrated tip

Brilliant Breads

Soups

Salads

English Muffins

Starter
1¹/2 cups all-purpose flour
¹/8 teaspoon instant dry yeast
³/4 cup water

Muffins
1³/4 cups all-purpose flour
1 teaspoon instant dry yeast
2 tablespoons cornstarch
2 tablespoons diastatic malt powder
  or brown sugar
1 teaspoon baking powder
2 teaspoons kosher salt
1 egg, lightly beaten
2 teaspoons cider vinegar
1 tablespoon unsalted butter, melted
³/4 cup milk, warmed
2 tablespoons semolina for sprinkling

You can make these muffins a day ahead and cool to room temperature. Freeze them in a plastic bag and allow them to come to room temperature before cutting.

Special kitchen equipment
stand mixer; ten to twelve English muffin rings (optional); baking parchment

Starter

1 Combine the flour, yeast and water in a medium bowl and mix to form a smooth batter. Cover with a kitchen towel and let stand at room temperature for 4 to 16 hours; the mixture should be spongy and full of holes.

Muffins

2 Combine the starter with the flour, yeast, cornstarch, malt powder, baking powder and kosher salt in a stand mixer. Add the egg, vinegar, butter and milk and mix well. Beat for 5 to 8 minutes or until smooth. Let stand, covered, in a warm place for 1 hour or until doubled in bulk.

3 Oil ten to twelve English muffin rings lightly or spray with nonstick baking spray. Line a baking sheet with baking parchment and sprinkle with some of the semolina. Arrange the rings on the sheet. Stir the muffin dough and drop a scant ¹/4 cup dough into each ring. Sprinkle with additional semolina. Smooth with damp fingers if desired. Cover with a kitchen towel and let rise in a warm place for 1 hour.

4 Place a second baking sheet on top of the muffins to keep the tops flat during baking. Bake in a preheated 350-degree oven for 25 minutes or until light brown on both sides. Split with a fork and serve immediately or toast for a crunchier muffin.

Variation: For Dry-Fry Muffins, let the batter rise for 1¹/2 hours or until very puffy. Heat a griddle to 325 degrees, medium-hot. Place the lightly oiled muffin rings on the griddle and fill one-third full. Dry-fry the muffins for 10 to 12 minutes and then turn them over. Dry-fry on the other side for 5 to 6 minutes or until brown. Cool on a wire rack.

English Muffin Bread

1 Combine the milk, water, canola oil, and vinegar in the large bowl of a stand mixer fitted with a paddle. Add the bread flour, potato flour, yeast, sugar, kosher salt, malt powder and ascorbic acid. Mix until an elastic dough is formed. Place the dough in a large oiled bowl and turn to coat the surface. Let stand in a draft-free place until doubled in bulk.

2 Deflate the dough by lifting it gently from the bottom in a circular pattern and letting it fall back into the bowl. Shape into a tight loaf and place in a lightly greased loaf pan. Cover with plastic wrap and let rise in the refrigerator for 8 to 12 hours.

3 Let the dough stand at room temperature for 30 minutes or longer. Bake in a preheated 350-degree oven for 50 minutes or until the loaf tests done. Test by placing the tip of a thermometer into the center of the loaf after the crust begins to color; the temperature should read 196 to 198 degrees. Cool in the pan on a wire rack for 3 to 4 minutes. Remove the loaf from the pan and place on its side on a wire rack to cool completely.

Makes 1 large loaf

1 cup milk, slightly warmed
1/2 cup water, slightly warmed
2 tablespoons canola oil
1 tablespoon cider vinegar
3 1/2 cups bread flour
1 teaspoon potato flour
1 1/2 teaspoons instant dry yeast
1 1/2 teaspoons sugar
1 1/2 teaspoons kosher salt
1 teaspoon diastatic malt powder
1/8 teaspoon ascorbic acid (vitamin C)

The basic recipe for this was given to me by the King Arthur Flour Company. I have added my own embellishments along the way. It is great for toasting and especially good with my homemade Lemon Curd (page 120). Remember that the slower the rise, the better the texture will be.

Special kitchen equipment
stand mixer fitted with a paddle attachment; thermometer

Easy Croissants

Makes 16 large croissants or 32 small croissants

1 cup all-purpose flour
1/3 cup sugar
11/2 teaspoons instant dry yeast
1 egg, beaten
1 cup warm water
1 (5-ounce) can evaporated milk
1/4 cup (1/2 stick) butter, melted
3 cups all-purpose flour
1 cup (2 sticks) butter, chilled and
   cut into 1/4-inch pieces
11/2 teaspoons salt
11/2 cups all-purpose flour
1 egg
1 tablespoon cold water

1 Mix 1 cup flour, the sugar, yeast and one egg in a one-quart bowl. Combine the warm water and evaporated milk in a medium saucepan. Heat to 106 degrees. Add to the flour mixture and whisk until smooth. Whisk in 1/4 cup melted butter.

2 Combine 3 cups flour, 1 cup chilled butter and the salt in a food processor fitted with a steel blade. Pulse ten to fifteen times to form crumbs the size of kidney beans. Remove to a large bowl and stir in 11/2 cups flour. Add the yeast mixture and mix with a wooden spoon to form a dough. Chill, covered, for 4 hours or up to 3 days.

3 Knead the dough six times on a lightly floured work surface. Divide into two equal portions. Roll one portion at a time into a 15-inch circle on a floured work surface; keep the remaining dough covered in the refrigerator until needed. Cut the circle into eight wedges. Roll the wedges from the wide end, pulling slightly on the wide ends as you roll. Place 11/2 inches apart on an ungreased baking sheet lined with baking parchment paper and curve the ends to form crescents. Cover loosely with plastic wrap and let stand in a warm place for 11/2 hours or until doubled in bulk.

4 Beat one egg with the cold water in a small bowl. Strain into a second bowl and brush over the croissants with a pastry brush. Bake at 350 degrees for 20 to 25 minutes or until golden brown. Serve warm.

After rolling the dough into wedges, you can cut a 1-inch slit in the center of the wide end to give the points more give and make the croissants look more relaxed. You can freeze the unbaked croissants on the baking sheet and store in a large plastic freezer bag. Thaw the desired number on a baking sheet in the refrigerator. Let stand in a warm place for 11/2 hours or until doubled in bulk and bake as directed.

Special kitchen equipment
food processor; pastry brush;
   baking parchment

Brioche Cinnamon Rolls

Makes 12 rolls

Rolls

1/2 recipe Brioche dough (page 32)
2 tablespoons unsalted butter, softened
2 tablespoons cinnamon-sugar
1/2 cup chopped pecans, toasted (optional)

Caramel Cream

3/4 cup granulated or baker's sugar
2 or 3 drops of lemon juice
1/4 cup water
1/4 cup (about) cream, heated

You can cool the rolls to room temperature and store in an airtight container for up to 7 days. Reheat in a paper bag at 350 degrees for 10 minutes.

Special kitchen equipment

baking parchment; pastry brush

Rolls

1 Roll the Brioche dough to a 12×12-inch square on a lightly floured work surface. Spread the butter over the entire surface. Mix the cinnamon-sugar and pecans in a small bowl. Sprinkle over the butter. Roll up the dough to enclose the filling and press the seams to seal. Cut into twelve slices.

2 Arrange the slices cut side down on a baking sheet lined with baking parchment. Bake in a preheated 350-degree oven for 30 minutes or until golden brown.

Caramel Cream

3 Combine the sugar, lemon juice and water in a small heavy saucepan. Heat over medium-high heat until the sugar dissolves, stirring constantly. Wet a pastry brush in warm water and brush the inside of the saucepan. Repeat the process two more times. Cover the saucepan and bring to a simmer over medium-high heat.

4 Reduce the heat to low and cook, uncovered, until the mixture is light golden brown. Remove from the heat and add the hot cream in a fine stream, mixing until smooth. Drizzle over the rolls. Cool slightly to serve.

Classic Bran Muffins

1 Sift the flour, baking powder, baking soda and salt together in a medium bowl. Stir in the wheat bran, wheat germ and raisins and mix well. Combine the canola oil, sugar, molasses, egg and milk in a bowl. Add to the flour mixture and mix well.

2 Spoon the batter into paper-lined muffin cups. Bake in a preheated 375-degree oven for 18 to 22 minutes or just until the muffins are set; do not overbake. Remove from the muffin cups and serve immediately or cool on a wire rack. You can freeze the muffins and store them in the freezer in airtight plastic bags for up to one month.

Note: This is my version of the recipe that the Canola Board gave to attendees at the 2006 annual IACP meeting. It has been adapted for high altitude.

Makes 6 medium or 12 miniature muffins

1/2 cup all-purpose flour
1/4 teaspoon (heaping) baking powder
1/8 teaspoon baking soda
1/4 teaspoon salt
1/2 cup wheat bran
1/4 cup wheat germ
1/2 cup golden raisins or dried fruit
2 tablespoons canola oil
1/4 cup sugar
2 tablespoons mild molasses
1 egg, beaten
1/2 cup milk

Special kitchen equipment
muffin tins; paper liners

Honey Wheat Loaf

1 Combine the milk, water, butter and honey in the large bowl of a stand mixer; mix well. Add the whole wheat flour, unbleached flour, potato flour, wheat gluten, yeast, kosher salt, malt powder and ascorbic acid and mix with a dough hook for 15 minutes to form an elastic dough.

2 Remove the dough to a large greased bowl and turn to coat the surface. Let stand, covered, in a warm place free of drafts until doubled in bulk. Deflate the dough by lifting it from the bottom in a circular pattern and letting it fall back into the bowl. Knead the dough very lightly and shape into a tight loaf. Place in a lightly greased loaf pan. Cover with plastic wrap and let rise in the refrigerator for 8 hours or longer.

3 Let the loaf stand at room temperature for 30 minutes or longer. Bake the loaf in a preheated 350-degree oven for 45 minutes or until golden brown. Place the tip of a thermometer in the center of the loaf after the crust begins to color; the temperature should read 196 to 198 degrees.

Note: You can substitute 1 1/2 cups all-purpose flour for the unbleached flour to lighten the bread.

Makes 1 large loaf

1 cup milk, slightly warmed
1/2 cup water, slightly warmed
2 tablespoons butter, softened
1 tablespoon honey
2 cups whole wheat flour
1 1/2 cups unbleached flour
1 teaspoon potato flour
1 tablespoon vital wheat gluten
1 teaspoon instant dry yeast
1 1/2 teaspoons kosher salt
1 teaspoon diastatic malt powder
1/8 teaspoon ascorbic acid (vitamin C)

Special kitchen equipment
*stand mixer fitted with a dough hook;
    thermometer*

Focaccia with Olives

Makes one 10-inch loaf

Sponge

1 cup unbleached flour
1 tablespoon sugar
1 teaspoon instant dry yeast
1/2 cup warm (100-degree) water

Focaccia

2 1/2 cups unbleached flour
1 1/2 teaspoons salt
1/3 cup olive oil
1/3 cup pinot grigio or other dry white wine
1/4 cup warm water (100 degrees)
1/4 cup coarsely chopped black olives
1 tablespoon fresh rosemary leaves, chopped
Olive oil for sprinkling

Focaccia originated in Genoa, but many variations on the classic Genoese hearth bread are found all over Liguria. This recipe calls for the olives, the olive oil, and, especially, the white wine of the region to add another flavor dimension. It is best served slightly warm.

Special kitchen equipment

heavy baking pan with low sides (cast-iron is ideal)

Sponge

1 Combine the flour, sugar and yeast in a medium bowl. Add the warm water and mix to form a soft paste. Cover the bowl and let rise for 20 minutes or until frothy.

Focaccia

2 Combine the flour and salt in a large bowl. Make a well in the center and add the sponge, 1/3 cup olive oil and the wine. Stir to combine. Add enough water to form a soft, sticky dough.

3 Knead the dough on a lightly floured work surface for 10 minutes or until smooth and elastic. Separate out about one-fourth of the dough and knead in the olives and rosemary. Knead the portion into the whole batch of dough. Knead with a stand mixer fitted with a paddle if you prefer. Place in an oiled bowl and turn to coat the surface.

4 Let rise, covered with a dish towel, for 1 1/2 to 2 hours or until doubled in bulk. Deflate the dough by removing it to a lightly floured surface. Move it gently in a circular motion with cupped hands for 5 minutes. Let rest for 10 minutes. Professional bread bakers use this technique to help develop the crumb, or the interior texture of the loaf defined by its hole structure or webbing.

5 Pat the dough to a 9 1/2-inch circle 1/2 inch thick on a lightly floured work surface. Place on an oiled heavy baking pan and cover with plastic wrap. Let rise for 1 hour in a warm place or for longer in the refrigerator until doubled in bulk.

6 Press indentations 1/2 inch deep in the surface with your fingertips. Bake in a preheated 400-degree oven for 30 minutes or until golden brown and hollow sounding when tapped. Sprinkle with additional olive oil. Remove to a wire rack to cool.

Wine and Black Pepper Cracker Bread

1 Stir together the flour, sugar, yeast, baking powder, kosher salt and pepper in a large bowl. Combine the wine, buttermilk and butter in a small microwave-safe bowl. Microwave just until the butter melts. Add to the dry ingredients and mix to form a smooth soft dough, adding additional flour if the dough is too sticky.

2 Knead on a lightly floured work surface for 5 minutes or until smooth and elastic, pushing away with the heel of your hand and drawing the dough together in a ball; knead with a stand mixer fitted with a dough hook if you prefer.

3 Shape into a ball and place in an oiled bowl, turning to coat the surface. Cover with a damp kitchen towel and let rise in a warm place for 1 to 1½ hours or until doubled in bulk.

4 Remove the dough to a generously floured work surface and work lightly to release the air. Divide into four portions. Roll one portion at a time through the widest setting of a pasta machine, leaving the remaining portions covered until needed. Fold the dough and roll it again. Repeat the process six to eight times or until the dough is firm and elastic, adjusting the machine to finer settings until the dough is rolled very thin. Place the thin strips on a work surface and cut into long, pointed wedges.

5 Place the wedges on baking sheets lined with baking parchment. Prick the wedges all over with a fork to ensure even rising. Bake one sheet at time in a preheated 375-degree oven for 7 to 10 minutes or until light brown. Remove to a wire rack to cool. Store in an airtight container for up to one week.

Makes 50 to 60 crisp bread wedges

1½ cups (or more) all-purpose flour
1 teaspoon sugar
1 teaspoon instant dry yeast
½ teaspoon baking powder
½ teaspoon kosher salt
1 teaspoon freshly ground
*   black pepper*
⅓ cup dry white wine
⅓ cup buttermilk
2 tablespoons unsalted butter

This is my version of a cracker bread from Anne Willan, founder of La Varenne French cooking school.

Special kitchen equipment
hand-cranked or electric pasta machine; pastry cutter or pizza wheel; baking parchment

Cream of Portobello Mushroom Soup with Puff Pastry

Makes 6 servings

1 Scrape off the gills from the mushrooms with a grapefruit spoon with a serrated tip. Quarter and thinly slice the mushrooms. Heat the butter in a heavy saucepan over medium-high heat. Add the mushrooms and onions and season with kosher salt and pepper. Sauté until the vegetables are tender and all the liquid from the mushrooms has evaporated, stirring occasionally.

2 Add the stock and cream. Reduce the heat and simmer for 15 minutes. Pour half the mixture into a heatproof bowl and purée with an immersion blender. Stir the purée and wine into the soup remaining in the saucepan. Cook until heated through. Season with additional kosher salt and pepper. Let stand until cool. Pour into six ovenproof bowls 3 to 4 inches in diameter. Stir the sliced chives into each bowl.

3 Roll one sheet of the puff pastry at a time on a work surface. Cut circles about 1/2 inch larger in diameter than the bowls using a pizza cutter. Brush the outer edges of the circles with the beaten egg. Invert the pastry with the egg side down over the soup bowl and press to seal to the bowl. Brush the tops with additional egg. Chill for 1 to 24 hours.

4 Place the bowls on a baking sheet. Bake in a preheated 400-degree oven for 30 minutes or until the pastry is golden brown. Serve immediately.

1 1/2 pounds portobello mushrooms
2 tablespoons unsalted butter
2 onions, minced
Kosher salt and pepper to taste
3 cups chicken stock or
    vegetable stock
1 cup cream
2 tablespoons dry sherry
1/4 cup thinly sliced fresh chives
2 sheets frozen puff pastry,
    thawed and chilled, or
    Classic Puff Pastry (page 118)
1 egg, beaten

This soup is several steps above comfort food. It can be easily made any time of the year with just a few ingredients. If you are up to it, start the day before and make homemade Puff Pastry.

Special kitchen equipment
grapefruit spoon with a serrated tip; immersion blender or food processor; six ovenproof bowls; pizza cutter

Artichoke Cream Soup

2 tablespoons olive oil
2 shallots, sliced
1 (14-ounce) package frozen artichoke
    quarters, thawed
2 cups vegetable stock or chicken stock
1/4 cup (1/2 stick) butter, softened
1/3 cup heavy cream
3 garlic cloves, roasted and mashed
Salt and freshly ground pepper to taste
6 tablespoons olive oil
1 medium russet potato, peeled
    and julienned

Special kitchen equipment
Blender; fine-mesh strainer

1 Heat 2 tablespoon olive oil in a large sauté pan. Add the shallots and sauté until translucent. Add three-fourths of the artichokes and the vegetable stock. Simmer for 20 minutes or until the artichokes are tender.

2 Pour the mixture into a blender and add the butter, cream, garlic, salt and pepper. Process until smooth. Pour through a fine-mesh strainer into a saucepan and keep warm.

3 Heat 2 tablespoons of the olive oil in a large heavy skillet over medium-high heat. Add the remaining one-fourth of the artichokes. Pan-roast for 10 to 15 minutes or until golden brown.

4 Heat the remaining 4 tablespoons olive oil in a medium sauté pan. Add the potato and fry until light golden brown; drain on paper towels. Ladle the soup into soup bowls and top with the potato croutons and pan-roasted artichokes.

Asparagus Cream Soup with Herb Crème Fraîche

3 pounds fresh asparagus
2 tablespoons Clarified Butter (page 117)
4 shallots, thinly sliced
1/8 teaspoon kosher salt
Pinch of ascorbic acid (vitamin C)
Pinch of kosher salt
4 cups chicken stock, warmed
Freshly ground white pepper to taste
Kosher salt to taste
Herb Crème Fraîche (page 116)

Special kitchen equipment
immersion blender

1 Snap off the tough ends of the asparagus spears and chop or break the spears into 1-inch pieces. Melt the Clarified Butter in a heavy saucepan over very low heat. Add the shallots and 1/8 teaspoon kosher salt. Simmer, covered, for 5 minutes or until the shallots are tender. Add the asparagus, ascorbic acid and a pinch of kosher salt. Simmer, covered, for 10 minutes or until the asparagus is almost tender.

2 Add the heated chicken stock to the saucepan and increase the heat to a low simmer. Simmer, covered, for 15 minutes or until the asparagus is very tender. Purée the mixture with an immersion blender. Season with white pepper and additional kosher salt if needed.

3 Ladle the soup into soup bowls and top each serving with a large dollop of Herb Crème Fraîche, swirling it if desired.

Note: The pinch of ascorbic acid helps retain the green color of the asparagus. You can prepare the soup two to three days in advance and reheat it gently to serve.

Chilled Cucumber and Avocado Soup with Spicy Glazed Shrimp

Makes 6 servings

1 Combine the cucumber, avocados, buttermilk, vinegar, sugar, lime juice and salt in a blender; process until smooth. Pour through a fine-mesh strainer into a large bowl. Chill for 40 minutes.

2 Ladle the soup into soup bowls. Place two or three Glazed Shrimp on top and drizzle with the glaze from the shrimp. Garnish each with a mint leaf.

1 large English cucumber, chopped
2 Hass avocados, chopped
1 1/2 cups buttermilk
2 tablespoons red wine vinegar
1 teaspoon sugar
1 1/2 teaspoons fresh lime juice
Pinch of salt
Spicy Glazed Shrimp (below)
6 mint leaves, for garnish

Special kitchen equipment
Blender; fine-mesh strainer

Spicy Glazed Shrimp

Makes 6 servings

1 Peel and devein the shrimp, reserving the shells. Heat 2 tablespoons canola oil in a large saucepan over medium heat. Add the shrimp shells, garlic, shallot and carrot. Cook for 8 minutes or until the shrimp shells are light brown and the vegetables are tender, stirring constantly. Add the coriander seeds, cumin seeds, peppercorns and crushed red pepper. Sauté for 1 minute.

2 Stir in the tomato paste and cook for 1 minute, stirring constantly. Add the water, honey and lime juice. Bring to a boil and reduce the heat to medium-low. Simmer for 15 minutes or until the liquid is reduced to 1/2 cup. Pour through a fine-mesh strainer into a heatproof bowl.

3 Heat 1 tablespoon canola in a medium skillet over high heat until shimmering. Add the shrimp and season with salt and black pepper. Cook for 1 minute. Turn the shrimp over and add the glaze. Simmer for 2 minutes or just until the shrimp are cooked through. Swirl in the butter.

6 ounces unpeeled large shrimp
2 tablespoons canola oil
3 garlic cloves, thinly sliced
1 shallot, thinly sliced
1 small carrot, thinly sliced
1 teaspoon coriander seeds
1/2 teaspoon cumin seeds
1 teaspoons black peppercorns
1 teaspoon crushed red pepper
1 teaspoon tomato paste
2 cups water
1 tablespoon honey
1 tablespoon lime juice
1 tablespoon canola oil
Salt and freshly ground black pepper to taste
1 tablespoon unsalted butter (optional)

Special kitchen equipment
fine-mesh strainer

Cream of Mussel Soup

Makes 6 servings

Mussels
1 pound mussels
1/3 cup dry white wine
2 sprigs parsley
1 sprig thyme
1/2 bay leaf
1 teaspoon minced shallots

Soup
1 tablespoon butter
1/2 teaspoon fennel seeds
3 cups sliced onions
1 teaspoon curry powder
1/3 cup dry white wine
1/3 cup (or more) tomato juice or
  vegetable juice cocktail
13/4 cups canned tomatoes
1 sprig thyme
1/2 bay leaf
6 saffron threads
11/2 cups heavy cream
3 tablespoons Pernod
1 strip orange zest
Salt and cayenne pepper to taste

Special kitchen equipment
food processor; fine-mesh strainer

Mussels

1 Discard any mussels that have broken shells or that are not tightly closed. Combine the wine, parsley, thyme, bay leaf and shallots in a saucepan large enough to hold the mussels when they open. Bring to a boil and add the mussels. Cover and steam for 3 minutes or until the mussels open. Discard any mussels that do not open.

2 Remove the mussels to a bowl with a slotted spoon. Strain the cooking liquid through a fine-mesh strainer into a bowl and reserve. Remove the mussels from their shells and reserve.

Soup

3 Melt the butter in a large saucepan over medium heat. Add the fennel seeds and sauté for 1 minute. Add the onions and curry powder. Sauté for 5 minutes or until the onions are tender and translucent. Stir in the wine, tomato juice, tomatoes, thyme, bay leaf and saffron. Simmer for 30 minutes, stirring occasionally.

4 Remove the bay leaf. Process the soup in batches in a food processor. Combine the batches in the saucepan and add the reserved mussels and reserved cooking liquid. Simmer for 10 minutes. Strain through a fine-mesh strainer into a bowl, pressing the mussels lightly to extract all the juices. Discard the mussels and return the soup to the saucepan.

5 Stir the cream and liqueur into the soup. Simmer for 5 minutes. Add the orange zest and simmer for 5 minutes. Remove the orange zest with a slotted spoon and season the soup with salt and cayenne pepper. Add additional tomato juice if needed for the desired consistency. Serve hot or cold as a starter or with a crisp salad as a light meal.

Note: You can prepare the soup ahead of time and chill in the refrigerator. It tastes great hot or cold.

Southwest Butternut Squash Soup

1 Mix the coriander, cumin, cinnamon, cayenne pepper and chili powder in a small bowl. Heat the Clarified Butter in a large heavy saucepan. Add the onions, carrots and jalapeño chiles and sauté until tender. Add the spice mixture and sauté over low heat for 2 minutes longer.

2 Add the squash, stock, orange juice and lime juice. Simmer for 30 minutes or until the squash is tender. Cool for several minutes. Purée with an immersion blenderor in a blender. Return to the saucepan and season with salt and pepper.

3 Cook just until heated through. Stir in the cream. Ladle into soup bowls and garnish each serving with a dollop of crème fraîche, toasted pumpkin seeds and cilantro leaves.

1 tablespoon coriander
1 1/2 teaspoons cumin
1/2 teaspoon cinnamon
1/2 teaspoon cayenne pepper
1/2 teaspoon chili powder
1/4 cup Clarified Butter (page 117)
2 large onions, chopped
2 carrots, peeled and chopped
2 jalapeño chiles, finely chopped
2 butternut squash, peeled and
    cut into 1/2-inch pieces
4 cups (or more) chicken stock
Juice of 2 oranges
Juice of 1 lime
Salt and pepper to taste
1 cup heavy cream (optional)
Crème Fraîche (page 116), for garnish
1 cup Spicy Toasted Pine Nuts
    (below) or toasted pumpkin seeds,
    for garnish
Leaves of 1/2 bunch cilantro,
    for garnish

Special kitchen equipment
immersion blender or blender

Spicy Toasted Pine Nuts

Makes 1 cup

Sauté the pine nuts with the cumin, chili powder, cayenne pepper, salt and black pepper in the canola oil in a skillet over high heat until crisp and fragrant. Cool to room temperature and store in an airtight container for up to 2 weeks.

1 cup unsalted unroasted pine nuts
1/2 teaspoon cumin
1/2 teaspoon chili powder
1/4 teaspoon cayenne pepper
Salt and black pepper to taste
2 tablespoons canola oil

Gazpacho

Makes 4 servings

2 tablespoons olive oil
4 (1/2-inch) slices day-old baguette
1/2 red bell pepper, seeded
1 English cucumber, peeled and seeded
1/2 red onion
3 large ripe tomatoes
1 cup tomato juice
1/4 cup sherry vinegar or cider vinegar
5 tablespoons olive oil
1 garlic clove, minced
1 small hot chile, seeded and chopped
Kosher salt and freshly ground pepper
    to taste
1 scallion, white and green portions, finely
    chopped, for garnish
2 tablespoons chopped cilantro or parsley,
    for garnish

Special kitchen equipment
food processor or blender

1 Heat 2 tablespoons olive oil in a small skillet over medium heat. Add the bread and cook for 2 minutes on each side or until toasted. Remove to a food processor or blender and pulse until coarsely chopped. Remove to a large bowl.

2 Chop the cucumber and bell pepper separately in the food processor by pulsing until coarsely chopped. Reserve 2 tablespoons each of the bell pepper and cucumber and add the rest to the bread in the bowl. Chop the onion and tomatoes separately in the food processor and add each to the bowl. Add the tomato juice, vinegar, 5 tablespoons olive oil, garlic, chile, salt and pepper. Taste and adjust the vinegar, salt and pepper as needed.

3 Chill the gazpacho for 1 hour or longer. Ladle into chilled bowls or glasses and top with the reserved cucumber and bell pepper. Garnish with the scallion and cilantro. Serve chilled.

Note: Gazpacho is a healthy summer lunch choice. I like a chunky texture with a spicy zing, but not hot. The longer the gazpacho chills, the better the flavors develop.

Cream of Potato and Leek Soup

Makes 6 servings

3 tablespoons unsalted butter
3 leeks, white portions only,
    finely chopped
2 pounds potatoes, peeled and
    cut into cubes
8 cups chicken stock
1 1/2 to 2 cups heavy cream
    (optional)
Salt and pepper to taste
Pinch of nutmeg
2 or 3 drops of lemon juice

Special kitchen equipment
immersion blender

1 Melt the butter in a saucepan over medium heat. Add the leeks and sauté until very tender. Add the potatoes and stock. Cook, covered, until the potatoes are very tender. Drain, reserving the cooking liquid.

2 Purée the potato mixture with an immersion blender. Add the cream and enough of the reserved cooking liquid to make a thick soup. Bring to a simmer over low heat and season with salt, pepper, nutmeg and lemon juice. Ladle into soup bowls and serve hot or chilled.

Black Bean Soup

1 Combine the beans with enough water to cover in a bowl for 2 hours or longer; drain.

2 Heat the canola oil in a 6-quart saucepan over medium-high heat. Add the onion and cumin and sauté until the onion is tender-crisp. Add 7 cups water, the beans, bacon, garlic and bay leaves.

3 Bring to a boil and reduce the heat. Cook uncovered at a low simmer for 1 hour or until the beans are tender, stirring occasionally and adding warm water as needed to cover the beans. Cook for a longer time at higher altitudes if necessary.

4 Discard the bay leaves and use an immersion blender to purée enough of the beans to thicken the soup and provide a cream base. Season with salt.

5 Ladle into soup bowls and stir in just enough of the lime juice to give it a zing and sharpen the flavors. Serve with the Mango Salsa.

Note: This is an easy make-ahead dish that is tasty with the Mango Salsa, but is also delicious served over hot rice or garnished with julienned Roma tomatoes.

Makes 8 servings

*1 pound dried black beans
    (about 2¹/2 cups), sorted
    and rinsed
1 tablespoon canola oil
1 cup finely chopped red onion
1¹/2 teaspoons cumin seeds, toasted
    and finely ground
7 cups (or more) warm water
4 slices smoked bacon, chopped
4 garlic cloves, sliced
2 large bay leaves
Salt to taste
1 to 2 tablespoons fresh lime juice
Mango Salsa (below)*

Special kitchen equipment
immersion blender

Mango Salsa

Combine the onion with ice water in a bowl and let stand for 5 minutes; drain. Add the mango, red bell pepper, jalapeño chile, ginger and cilantro; mix well. Stir in the lime juice, olive oil, honey and salt. Let stand for 30 minutes to develop the flavors. Store, covered, in the refrigerator for up to 2 days.

Makes 1¹/2 cups

*¹/4 cup finely chopped red onion
1 cup chopped firm mango
2 tablespoons finely chopped red
    bell pepper
1 teaspoon minced jalapeño chile
2 teaspoons minced peeled
    fresh ginger
2 tablespoons coarsely chopped
    fresh cilantro leaves
2 tablespoons fresh lime juice
2 teaspoons olive oil
Several drops of honey, or to taste
Salt to taste*

Roasted Beet Salad with Caviar and Vodka Gelée

Makes 6 servings

Orange Vinaigrette

1¹/3 cups fresh orange juice
¹/2 cup white wine vinegar
¹/2 cup olive oil
¹/4 cup walnut oil
3 tablespoons chopped tarragon
1 tablespoon minced shallots
1 teaspoon minced garlic
Salt and freshly ground pepper to taste

Roasted Beets

8 unpeeled red beets
4 unpeeled baby yellow beets
2/3 cup olive oil
1/3 cup balsamic vinegar
4 sprigs fresh rosemary
6 sprigs fresh thyme
1/4 cup Crème Fraîche (page 116)
1/4 cup domestic yellow caviar (optional)
Grated orange zest, for garnish
Sprigs of chervil or mint, for garnish
Vodka Gelée (page 47), for garnish

Roasting the beets brings out their natural sweetness and intensifies their flavor. For this dish, the beets can be roasted, plated and chilled until time to dress and garnish. The extravagant touches of caviar and Vodka Gelée are optional.

Special kitchen equipment

mandoline (adjustable slicer with a sharp blade, optional)

Vinaigrette

1 Combine the orange juice, vinegar, olive oil and walnut oil in a large stainless steel bowl. Add the tarragon, shallots, garlic, salt and pepper and whisk until smooth. Pour into a jar with a tight-fitting lid.

Roasted Beets

2 Rinse the beets in cold water and cut off the greens, leaving about 2 inches of the stems. Combine with the olive oil, vinegar, rosemary and thyme in a bowl and toss to coat well. Arrange in a single layer in a baking dish. Cover with foil.

3 Roast in a preheated 350-degree oven for 40 to 50 minutes or until the yellow beets are tender when pierced with the point of a sharp knife. Remove the yellow beets. Roast the red beets for 25 minutes longer or until tender.

4 Let the beets stand until cool enough to handle. Remove the peels with a small knife under running water. Cut the yellow beets into wedges. Slice the red beets 1/8 inch thick with a mandoline or sharp knife. Arrange the red beets in overlapping concentric circles on serving plates. Arrange the yellow beets over the red beets. Shake the vinaigrette to mix well and drizzle over the beets. Top with a dollop of Crème Fraîche and caviar. Garnish with a sprinkle of orange zest, chervil and Vodka Gelée.

Vodka Gelée

Makes 1 cup

1   Sprinkle the gelatin over the cool water in a bowl and let
stand until softened. Place the bowl in a small saucepan and
add enough warm water to reach halfway up the bowl. Bring to
a simmer over medium-high heat. Reduce the heat and simmer
until the gelatin dissolves, stirring constantly. Cool slightly.

2   Pour the gelatin into the vodka in a medium-small bowl; mix
well. Spoon into a 8×8-inch dish; the vodka mixture should
be about 1/2 inch deep. Chill until set. Cut into 1/2-inch cubes.

1 tablespoon unflavored gelatin
1/2 cup cool water
1/2 cup lemon-flavored vodka

Brie Triangles on Baby Greens

Makes 6 servings

1 (7-inch) wheel Brie cheese or
    Camembert cheese, chilled
2 sheets phyllo dough
1/4 cup melted Clarified Butter (page 117)
1 cup balsamic vinegar
1/4 cup Clarified Butter (page 117)
2 cups salad greens
1/4 cup Sherry Vinaigrette (below)
1/4 cup toasted pecans, for garnish

These little wedges of phyllo-wrapped cheese can be assembled well in advance and browned just before serving. When you cut into the pastry with a fork, the warm cheese oozes out onto the greens, creating a delightful surprise. The richness of the cheese is beautifully balanced with the tartness of the balsamic vinegar.

Special kitchen equipment
*pastry brush; baking parchment;
    long-handle tongs*

1   Cut the cheese wheel into six triangles. Layer the two sheets of phyllo dough on a work surface, using a pastry brush to brush each sheet with 2 tablespoons of the melted Clarified Butter. Cut the sheets into six strips about 2 1/2 inches wide with a sharp knife.

2   Place one triangle of cheese at the end of one phyllo strip and fold over to cover the cheese and form a triangle. Continue to fold the dough flag fashion, maintaining the triangular shape. Repeat with the remaining dough strips and cheese triangles. Arrange seam side down on a baking parchment-lined baking sheet. Chill, covered, in the refrigerator.

3   Bring the balsamic vinegar to a simmer in a small heavy saucepan. Cook until the vinegar is reduced by one-half.

4   Heat 1/4 cup Clarified Butter in a large skillet over low heat until it begins to bubble. Add the cheese triangles and sauté for 30 to 45 seconds on each side or until golden brown. Remove from the skillet with long-handle tongs and drain on paper towels.

5   Combine the salad greens with the Sherry Vinaigrette in a large bowl and toss to coat well. Spoon the greens onto six serving plates and place one warm cheese triangle on each plate. Drizzle the reduced balsamic vinegar around the plate and garnish with the pecans.

Sherry Vinaigrette

Makes 3 cups

1 1/2 tablespoons dry sherry
2/3 cup sherry vinegar
1 cup vegetable oil
2/3 cup olive oil
1/4 cup walnut oil
2 tablespoons Dijon mustard
1 1/2 teaspoons minced shallot
1/2 teaspoon minced garlic
Kosher salt and freshly ground pepper
    to taste

Whisk the sherry, sherry vinegar, vegetable oil, olive oil, walnut oil and Dijon mustard together in a medium bowl. Add the shallots and garlic and whisk until smooth. Season with kosher salt and pepper. Spoon into a jar with a tight-fitting lid and store in the refrigerator. Shake well before using.

Dijon-Poached Chicken with Apple and Blue Cheese Salad

1 Combine the water, wine, Dijon mustard, celery, onion, tarragon, bay leaf, kosher salt and peppercorns in a large saucepan. Bring to a boil and reduce the heat to a low simmer. Cook for 35 to 40 minutes.

2 Add the chicken. Cover and cook for 10 to 12 minutes or until the chicken is completely opaque. Remove with long-handle tongs to a plate and let stand until cool; discard the liquid or reserve for another use. Cut the chicken into thin slices.

3 Slice the apple and combine with the lemon juice and enough water to cover in a bowl. Toss the greens with Dijon Vinaigrette in a bowl. Arrange the sliced chicken over the greens. Drain the apples and pat dry with paper towels. Arrange over the greens and sprinkle with the walnuts and blue cheese.

Note: Wine is used in both the poaching liquid and vinaigrette in this dish. Enjoy it with a fruity riesling or crisp pinot gris or pinot grigio.

Makes 6 to 8 main-dish servings

2 cups water
1 cup dry white wine
1 tablespoon Dijon mustard
1/2 cup chopped celery
1 yellow onion, thickly sliced
2 sprigs tarragon
1 dried bay leaf
1/2 teaspoon kosher salt
1/2 teaspoon black peppercorns
4 boneless skinless chicken breasts
1 Granny Smith apple, peeled
Juice of 1/2 lemon
5 to 6 cups torn salad greens
Dijon Vinaigrette (below)
1 cup coarsely chopped walnuts, toasted
4 ounces blue cheese, crumbled

Special kitchen equipment
long-handle tongs

Dijon Vinaigrette

Whisk the Champagne, honey, vinegar, water and Dijon mustard together in a small bowl. Add the shallots and tarragon and whisk until smooth. Whisk in enough olive oil to produce the desired consistency. Season with salt and pepper.

Makes about 11/2 to 12/3 cups

1 cup Champagne or dry white wine
1/4 cup honey
1/4 cup white wine vinegar
1/4 cup water
1 tablespoon Dijon mustard
1 tablespoon minced shallots
1 tablespoon minced tarragon
1/2 to 3/4 cup olive oil
Salt and pepper to taste

Brilliant Salads

49

Seared Scallops with Chanterelles and Hearty Greens

Makes 4 to 8 servings

16 large sea scallops (1 to 1^1/$_4$ pounds)
^{1}/$_2$ teaspoon kosher salt
Coarsely ground white pepper to taste
2 tablespoons canola oil
2 tablespoons Clarified Butter (page 117)
4 chanterelles, sliced
1 shallot, thinly sliced
Kosher salt to taste
1 leaf radicchio, julienned
^{1}/$_2$ head endive, julienned
1 leaf escarole, inner portion only, julienned
^{1}/$_2$ teaspoon chopped fresh marjoram
^{1}/$_2$ cup dry white wine
^{1}/$_4$ cup (^{1}/$_2$ stick) Clarified Butter (page 117)

1 Pat the scallops dry with paper towels and season well with ^{1}/$_2$ teaspoon kosher salt and white pepper. Let stand until room temperature. Heat the canola oil in a large sauté pan over medium-high heat until very hot. Add the scallops to the oil in a single layer with space between them. Sear the scallops without moving them for 2 to 3 minutes or until well browned on the bottom. Remove to a warm platter and cover loosely with foil to keep warm.

2 Add 2 tablespoons Clarified Butter to the sauté pan and heat until bubbly. Add the mushrooms and shallot; sprinkle with additional kosher salt and white pepper. Sauté over medium-high heat for 4 minutes, tossing and stirring constantly. Add the radicchio, endive, escarole and marjoram and toss to mix well. Sauté for 2 minutes or until the greens are wilted. Stir in the wine and bring to a boil. Cook until most of the liquid evaporates, stirring occasionally.

3 Add ^{1}/$_4$ cup Clarified Butter to the sauté pan and stir to mix well. Add the scallops and cook until heated through. Adjust the seasonings if necessary. Spoon the mushroom mixture onto four to eight serving plates and top with the scallops. Serve immediately.

Note: The natural sweetness of the scallops is paired with the woodsy earthiness of the chanterelles and the natural bitterness of the greens in this dish. Serve it in the late summer or fall when the mushrooms are at their best. You can substitute dried mushrooms if fresh mushrooms are not available.

Avocado and Grapefruit Salad with Smoked Salmon

1 Combine the vermouth with salt and pepper in a medium bowl and whisk to mix well. Whisk in the canola oil gradually. Add the avocado slices and mix gently; do not mash the avocado.

2 Remove the zest from the grapefruit in thin strips and julienne the strips. Combine with boiling water in a saucepan and blanch for 2 minutes; drain well. Peel the white pith from the grapefruit and remove the sections with a serrated grapefruit knife.

3 Line individual serving plates with the arugula. Arrange the grapefruit sections and avocado slices in a flower pattern on the arugula, reserving the dressing. Arrange the smoked salmon in the center of the flower pattern and spoon the reserved dressing over the top. Garnish with the zest and serve at room temperature.

Makes 4 servings

1/2 cup white vermouth
Salt and pepper to taste
1/2 cup canola oil
2 avocados, sliced lengthwise
2 pink grapefruit
1 cup arugula, coarsely shredded
4 ounces smoked salmon,
    cut into strips

The splash of white vermouth binds this salad together in fine style. Serving it at room temperature awakens the taste buds.

Special kitchen equipment
serrated grapefruit knife

Exceptional Mains

Makes 6 servings

6 (4-ounce) pork tenderloin fillets
Kosher salt to taste
1 tablespoon Clarified Butter (page 117)
1 tablespoon vegetable oil
8 ounces goat cheese, at room temperature
1/4 cup Clarified Butter (page 117)
1 (8-ounce) package frozen phyllo dough,
   thawed in the package
1/4 cup minced chives

This is a magnificent main dish for guests as well as family. Use fillets from near the tail of the tenderloin so they are tall and narrow rather than short and wide.

Special kitchen equipment
pastry brush; thermometer

Individual Pork en Croûte with Goat Cheese and Mushrooms

1 Season the fillets generously on all sides with kosher salt. Heat 1 tablespoon Clarified Butter with the oil in a 10-inch skillet or sauté pan over medium heat until very hot and sizzling. Place three of the fillets in the skillet and sear for 1 to 2 minutes or until well browned. Turn the fillets and brown the other side. Sear the edges for 1 minute on each side, turning with tongs. Remove to a plate lined with paper towels and repeat with the remaining fillets. Cover and chill for 1 hour or longer.

2 Mash the goat cheese with a fork in a bowl until smooth. Melt 1/4 cup Clarified Butter over low heat in a small saucepan. Remove twenty-four sheets of phyllo dough from the package and trim them into 10-inch squares; discard the excess. Cover the sheets with plastic wrap until needed to prevent their drying out.

3 Place one square of dough on a dry work surface and brush lightly with the melted Clarified Butter. Sprinkle with about 1/2 teaspoon of the chives. Repeat the process with a second and third sheet of dough, placing each at a 90-degree angle over the previous sheet. Top with a fourth sheet to form a star-like design, brushing it with Clarified Butter.

4 Blot one pork fillet dry with a paper towel and place in the center of the star. Spread about 2 tablespoons of the goat cheese over the fillet and top with 2 tablespoons of the Mushroom Filling.

5 Gather up the points of the star one at a time, working around the star to form a packet or beggar's purse. Pinch the gathered dough lightly together close to the surface of the fillet and spread the points open slightly. Brush the entire surface of the packet, including the bottom, with Clarified Butter. Place on a heavy baking sheet. Repeat with the remaining dough and fillets.

6 Chill the packets, uncovered, for up to 8 hours. Let stand at room temperature for 20 minutes before baking.

7 Place an oven rack in the lower one-third of the oven. Bake the packets in a preheated 400-degree oven until a thermometer inserted through the side of the packet into the center of the fillet registers 155 degrees, rotating the baking sheet after 10 minutes to ensure even browning. The pork will continue to cook after it is removed from the oven. Serve immediately.

Mushroom Filling

8 Trim the mushrooms close to the caps. Combine the caps with the shallots and garlic in a food processor. Pulse until chopped but not puréed, scraping the bowl as needed. Remove the mixture to the center of a clean dish towel or cheesecloth. Gather up the sides of the towel and twist over the sink to squeeze as much liquid as possible from the mixture.

9 Heat the butter with the olive oil in a 10-inch skillet or sauté pan over medium heat. Add the mushroom mixture and cover. Cook for 3 to 5 minutes or until very tender and fragrant, stirring occasionally; do not brown. Remove the cover and cook for 2 to 3 minutes longer or until the mixture is nearly dry. Stir in the cilantro and season with the kosher salt and pepper.

Note: This can be prepared while the pork fillets are chilling, or it can be prepared in advance and chilled for up to one week or frozen for up to two weeks.

Mushroom Filling

1 pound cremini mushrooms
2 shallots, cut into halves
1 garlic clove, cut into halves
2 tablespoons unsalted butter
1 tablespoon olive oil
1/4 cup minced fresh cilantro
    or parsley
1/2 teaspoon kosher salt
Freshly ground pepper to taste

Special kitchen equipment
food processor

Seared Beef Tenderloin Steaks with Pan Sauce

1 Heat the canola oil in a 12-inch sauté pan over medium-high heat. Add the steaks to the pan and sear for 2 to 3 minutes on each side. Remove the steaks to a warm platter and cover with foil to keep warm.

2 Pour the excess drippings from the pan, leaving only a thin film of oil. Add the shallots and sauté until tender but not brown.

3 Mix the Dijon mustard and wine in a small bowl. Add to the sauté pan and stir with a flat-edge wooden spoon to deglaze the pan, stirring up any browned bits from the bottom. Stir in the stock and cook until the sauce is thickened. Stir in 2 teaspoons parsley.

4 Remove from the heat and whisk in the butter. Season with salt and pepper. Garnish with additional parsley to serve.

Note: When I am in a hurry, this is a quick and reliable main dish. Serve it with steamed brown rice or basmati rice cooked in chicken stock.

Makes 4 servings

1 to 2 tablespoons canola oil
4 (4-ounce) center-cut tenderloin
    steaks
2 shallots, minced
1 tablespoon Dijon mustard
1/2 cup dry white wine
1 cup chicken stock, heated
2 teaspoons minced parsley
2 tablespoons unsalted butter
    (optional)
Salt and pepper to taste
Minced parsley, for garnish

Special kitchen equipment
flat-edge wooden spoon

Pork Tenderloin Medallions with Calvados Sauce

Makes 4 servings

1 tablespoon canola oil
1 pound pork tenderloin,
    cut into 4 medallions
Kosher salt and freshly ground pepper
    to taste
2 tablespoons unsalted butter
2 large shallots, minced
1/4 cup Calvados or Cognac
1/4 cup apple cider
1 teaspoon fresh thyme leaves
1/2 cup chicken stock
3 tablespoons unsalted butter
Celery Root and Apple Purée (below)
Small sprigs of rosemary, for garnish

Pinot noir goes wonderfully with pork and is light enough not to overwhelm the sauce. California has fine pinot noirs, and excellent bottles are also available from Oregon. White wines can also work with pork—try a dry chenin blanc.

Makes 4 servings

1 1/2 pounds celery root
2 1/2 pounds Gala apples, Empire apples
    or McIntosh apples
1/4 cup (1/2 stick) unsalted butter
1 teaspoon salt
1/2 cup heavy cream
1/8 teaspoon freshly grated nutmeg
Pinch of freshly ground white pepper

Special kitchen equipment
immersion blender

1. Heat the canola oil in a 12-inch sauté pan over medium-high heat until very hot. Season the pork medallions with kosher salt and pepper. Add to the sauté pan and sear for 5 minutes or until brown on both sides, turning once. Remove to a warm platter and cover with foil; let stand for 10 minutes.

2. Place the same skillet, without cleaning, over medium heat. Melt 2 tablespoons butter in the skillet and add the shallots. Sauté for 3 minutes or until tender but not brown. Remove the pan from the heat and stir in the liqueur.

3. Return the pan to medium-high heat and cook for 1 to 2 minutes or until the liqueur has nearly evaporated. Add the apple cider and thyme. Reduce the heat and simmer for 2 to 3 minutes or until the liquid is reduced by one-half. Add the stock and simmer for 5 minutes or until the sauce is golden brown and coats the back of a wooden spoon. Swirl in 3 tablespoons butter.

4. Spoon the Celery Root and Apple Purée into the center of each serving plate. Place the pork medallions on the purée and drizzle the sauce over the medallions and around the edge of the plate. Garnish with watercress.

Celery Root and Apple Purée

1. Peel the celery root and apples and cut them into 1-inch pieces. Melt the butter in a heavy 6- to 8-quart saucepan over low heat. Add the celery root and apples and stir to coat evenly with the butter. Season with the salt. Cover tightly and simmer for 50 to 60 minutes or until the celery root is tender, stirring occasionally.

2. Process the mixture with an immersion blender for 3 to 4 minutes or until puréed. Add the cream, nutmeg and white pepper and mix well. Reheat, covered, over medium heat for 5 minutes or until heated through.

Pan-Grilled Lamb Chops with Béarnaise Sauce

Makes 2 to 4 servings

Béarnaise Sauce
1/4 cup white wine vinegar
1/3 cup dry white wine
4 shallots, minced
2 tablespoons fresh tarragon leaves
4 white peppercorns, crushed
4 egg yolks, beaten
1 cup (2 sticks) unsalted butter, melted
1/4 teaspoon salt
Pinch of cayenne pepper

Lamb Chops
Salt to taste
4 thick lamb chops

Having the surface of the skillet very hot before adding the lamb helps to prevent sticking. The salt draws the juices from the meat's surface, adding proteins and sugars to the surface and reducing its moisture content for better browning.

Special kitchen equipment
stainless steel bowl or double boiler

Béarnaise Sauce

1 Combine the vinegar and wine in a nonreactive medium saucepan. Add the shallots, tarragon and peppercorns. Cook over medium heat until the liquid is reduced to 1/4 cup. Strain into a medium stainless steel bowl or double boiler. Whisk in the egg yolks.

2 Place the bowl over a saucepan of simmering water, taking care that the water does not touch the bottom of the bowl. Cook just until the egg yolk mixture begins to thicken, whisking constantly. Remove the bowl immediately and whisk until thickened to the desired consistency.

3 Remove the saucepan from the heat and add several ice cubes to the water to reduce the heat. Return the bowl to the saucepan and drizzle in the butter very gradually, whisking constantly. Whisk in the salt and cayenne pepper. Set the bowl in a shallow pan of warm water to keep warm.

Note: If the sauce appears about to break, remove it from the hot water and whisk until it cools or whisk in 1 teaspoon cold water.

Lamb Chops

4 Heat a heavy uncoated skillet almost to smoking over high heat. Sprinkle a thin layer of salt over the bottom of the skillet, covering completely. Place the lamb chops in the heated skillet and sear for 3 minutes. Turn the chops over and sear for 3 minutes longer or until beads of the juices can be seen coming through the surface crust. Serve immediately with Béarnaise Sauce.

Braised Chicken in Curry Sauce

1 Combine the soy sauce, vodka and egg yolk in a large bowl and mix well. Add the chicken and stir to coat evenly. Marinate in the refrigerator for 15 to 30 minutes.

2 Combine the yams with water to cover in a bowl to prevent discoloration. Mix the fish sauce and coconut milk in a small bowl. Chop the lemon grass, garlic, shallots, ginger, cilantro and peppers in a spice grinder or by hand and place in a small bowl.

3 Heat the canola oil in a large flat-bottom wok or nonstick skillet over high heat. Add the chicken and stir-fry for 2 minutes or until lightly seared. Add the lemon grass mixture and stir-fry for 2 minutes or until fragrant. Stir in the turmeric and Red Curry Paste and cook for 1 minute, stirring to coat the chicken well.

4 Drain the yams and add to the wok with the coconut milk mixture. Cook for 2 minutes. Add the stock and cover. Reduce the heat and simmer for 15 minutes or until the chicken is very tender, stirring occasionally. Serve over hot steamed basmati rice.

Note: Look for yams at an Asian market. This is a healthy low-fat main dish filled with flavor. It is quick to prepare and can be prepared a day in advance.

Makes 4 to 6 servings

2 tablespoons soy sauce
2 tablespoons vodka
1 egg yolk, beaten
2 pounds boneless skinless chicken
    thighs, cut into 1 1/2-inch pieces
8 ounces yams, light-fleshed sweet
    potatoes or low-starch potatoes,
    peeled and cut into 1/2-inch pieces
3 tablespoons fish sauce
1/4 cup unsweetened coconut milk,
    whisked until smooth
1 stalk lemon grass, tender inner
    portion only, thinly sliced
2 garlic cloves, sliced
3 shallots, sliced
1 tablespoon minced peeled fresh ginger
1 tablespoon chopped cilantro
3 fresh hot peppers, or
    1 dried hot pepper, seeded
1/4 cup canola oil
1/2 teaspoon turmeric
1 tablespoon Red Curry Paste
    (page 113)
1 cup chicken stock
Hot steamed basmati rice

An interesting dish with a little spice from the Thai Curry Sauce. A crisp, fruity wine such as a true rosé will complement this. Do not be confused by the well-known white zinfandels—instead, try some of the Italian rosés, which are crisp and show well with both the chicken and the sauce.

Special kitchen equipment
*spice grinder (optional); flat-bottom
    wok or large saucepan*

Roasted Chicken with Balsamic Pan Sauce

Makes 4 servings

1 lemon
$1/2$ cup ricotta cheese (optional)
3 tablespoons minced mixed herbs
1 ($3^1/2$-pound) roasting chicken
Olive oil for rubbing
Salt and pepper to taste
1 cup (or less) chicken stock
1 cup balsamic vinegar
2 tablespoons dark brown sugar

The roasting juices from the chicken mixed with the balsamic vinegar make a lively sauce to accompany the roasted chicken. The ricotta cheese mixture helps to keep the chicken moist.

Special kitchen equipment
roasting pan with low sides; thermometer

1 Grate the lemon zest into a small bowl, reserving the lemon. Stir in the ricotta cheese and herbs. Loosen the skin from the chicken with your fingers and pat the ricotta cheese mixture gently under the skin; pull the skin tightly to cover the cheese mixture well. Rub the chicken with olive oil and sprinkle salt and pepper into the cavity. Cut the reserved lemon into halves and squeeze the juice from each into the cavity. Place the lemon halves in the cavity.

2 Place the chicken in a roasting pan with low sides. Insert a thermometer in one of the legs where it fits snugly to the breast, but not allowing it to touch a bone. Roast in a preheated 400-degree oven for 1 hour or until the juices run clear and the thermometer registers 170 degrees. Remove the chicken to a large platter and cover loosely with foil to keep warm.

3 Strain the cooking juices from the roasting pan into a large measuring cup, discarding the solids. Skim and discard the fat from the surface of the pan juices and add enough stock to measure 1 cup.

4 Place the roasting pan over medium heat on two burners. Pour the vinegar into the pan and bring to a boil, scraping up the browned bits from the bottom of the pan. Pour into a saucepan.

5 Add the strained cooking liquid and brown sugar to the saucepan. Bring to a boil, whisking to dissolve the brown sugar. Cook for 10 minutes or until the mixture is reduced to $1^1/3$ cups and thinly coats the back of a wooden spoon. Season with salt and pepper. Spoon into a gravy boat. Slice the chicken and serve with the balsamic pan sauce.

Braised Game Hens with Fig and Pomegranate Sauce

1 Rub the game hens generously with canola oil and season with kosher salt and pepper. Heat 2 tablespoons canola oil in a large skillet over medium-high heat until the oil shimmers. Add the game hens in batches with the skin sides down; sear until brown; do not crowd the hens as this may steam them instead of searing.

2 Combine all the hens in a preheated large ovenproof skillet over medium-high heat; pieces may fit snugly in the skillet at this point. Add the stock, vinegar and pomegranate juice. Arrange the figs over and around the hens.

3 Cover the hens tightly with a piece of foil and then a lid. Place in a preheated 325-degree oven and braise for 45 to 55 minutes or until the hens are tender to the touch. Test for doneness with thermometer inserted in the thigh joint without allowing it to touch a bone; it should register 170 degrees. Remove the hens to a warm platter and cover loosely with foil; let stand for 5 minutes or longer.

4 Blend the flour with enough cold water to make a thick slurry. Add to the cooking liquid remaining in the skillet. Bring to a boil and cook until thickened, stirring constantly. Adjust the seasonings.

5 Spoon a large spoonful of steamed couscous into the center of each serving plate and arrange a game hen half over the couscous. Place several figs over the hens and drizzle with the sauce. Garnish with watercress and the lemon zest. Serve immediately with sautéed green beans or skillet-roasted asparagus and a tossed salad.

4 game hens, split into halves
Canola oil for rubbing
Kosher salt and freshly ground pepper to taste
2 tablespoons canola oil
1 cup chicken stock, heated
1/4 cup balsamic vinegar
1/4 cup pomegranate juice concentrate
12 dried figs, cut into quarters
2 tablespoons all-purpose flour
Steamed couscous
Watercress sprigs, for garnish
1 teaspoon grated lemon zest, for garnish

Syrah is the same grape as shiraz from Australia and Rhône wines from France. The fruit in it complements the fig and pomegranate sauce. This is an example of where a red wine goes with a white meat.

Special kitchen equipment
large ovenproof skillet; thermometer

Angel Hair Nests with Crab and Hazelnuts

Makes 6 servings

1 recipe fresh angel hair pasta
  (see Pasta Fresca, page 114)
1/4 cup olive oil
Grated zest of 1 lemon
2 garlic cloves, minced
1/4 cup minced parsley
Salt and freshly ground pepper to taste
1 tablespoon Clarified Butter (page 117)
1 tablespoon olive oil
5 garlic cloves, minced
3 shallots, minced
1 or 2 jalapeño chiles, julienned
8 ounces pasteurized crab meat,
  pressed to remove liquid
2 tablespoons minced parsley
2 tablespoons chopped toasted hazelnuts
Juice of 1/2 lemon
3 tablespoons coarse fresh bread crumbs
3 tablespoons unsalted butter

1 Cook the pasta al dente. Drain, but do not rinse. Combine with 1/4 cup olive oil, the lemon zest, two minced garlic cloves and 1/4 cup parsley in a bowl and mix to coat well. Season with salt and pepper.

2 Use a large fork to gather a serving of pasta and then twirl the strands to form the nest, or "haystack." Form six nests in a buttered baking dish.

3 Heat 1 tablespoon Clarified Butter and 1 tablespoon olive oil in a large sauté pan over medium heat. Add five minced garlic cloves, the shallots and jalapeño chile and sauté just until tender. Add the crab meat and cook just until heated through. Stir in 2 tablespoons parsley, the hazelnuts and lemon juice; season with salt and pepper.

4 Spoon the crab meat mixture into the pasta nests. Bake in a preheated 450-degree oven just until heated through. Sprinkle with the bread crumbs and dot with 3 tablespoons butter. Broil until golden brown. Serve immediately.

Twice-Baked Goat Cheese Soufflés

Makes 6 servings

Melted unsalted butter for brushing
Grated Parmesan cheese for coating
1/4 cup (1/2 stick) unsalted butter
1/4 cup all-purpose flour
1 1/2 cups milk, warmed
3/4 cup light cream or half-and-half
4 ounces soft goat cheese, mashed
1 tablespoon grated Parmesan cheese
2 tablespoons mixed chopped fresh herbs,
*   such as parsley, chives and tarragon*
3 egg yolks
Salt and freshly ground pepper to taste
4 egg whites
Pinch of cream of tartar
Softened unsalted butter for brushing
Fresh herbs, for garnish
Marinated cherry tomatoes, for garnish

The technique of baking the soufflés twice is different in that they are first baked in a water bath, creating a pudding-like consistency. Preheating the oven at a slightly lower temperature and then raising the temperature to a higher level allows the heat to give a bigger boost to the bottoms of the soufflés, and they will puff and rise higher.

Special kitchen equipment
six 4-ounce soufflé dishes or ramekins; pastry brush; stand mixer; six individual baking dishes

1 Coat the insides of six 4-ounce soufflé dishes with melted butter, using a pastry brush; coat lightly with Parmesan cheese. Chill in the refrigerator.

2 Melt 1/4 cup butter in a medium saucepan. Stir in the flour and cook over medium heat for 2 to 3 minutes or until smooth. Stir in the milk gradually and bring to a boil. Reduce the heat and simmer for 3 to 4 minutes, stirring constantly. Pour one-third of the mixture into a small saucepan. and pour the light cream over the top to prevent a skin from forming.

3 Add the goat cheese to the sauce remaining in the medium saucepan. Add 1 tablespoon Parmesan cheese and the chopped herbs. Remove from the heat and stir until smooth. Cool slightly. Add the egg yolks one at a time, mixing well after each addition. Season with salt and pepper.

4 Beat the eggs whites in a stand mixer until foamy. Add the cream of tartar and beat at high speed until stiff but not dry. Stir one-fourth of the egg whites into the cheese sauce in the medium saucepan, then fold in the remaining egg whites.

5 Spoon the mixture carefully into the prepared soufflé dishes. Smooth the tops even with the rims of the dishes with a metal spatula or knife. Make a groove in the top of each just inside the rim with your thumb. Place the dishes in a baking pan with sides and add enough boiling water to reach two-thirds of the way up the sides of the soufflé dishes.

6 Place on a rack in the lower two-thirds of a preheated 325-degree oven. Increase the oven temperature to 360 degrees. Bake for 25 to 30 minutes or until the soufflés are puffed and firm to the touch. Remove from the oven and let stand until cool to the touch.

7 Brush six individual baking dishes with softened butter. Loosen the soufflés from the sides of the soufflé dishes with a thin spatula and gently pull the soufflés from the sides. Invert the soufflés into the prepared dishes. Cover loosely with plastic wrap.

8 Increase the oven temperature to 375 degrees. Stir the remaining sauce to mix in the cream. Remove the plastic wrap and spoon the sauce over the soufflés, moistening well. Bake for 15 minutes or until puffed and golden brown. Garnish with fresh herbs and marinated cherry tomatoes. Serve immediately.

Gnocchi with Wild Mushrooms

2 tablespoons extra-virgin olive oil
2 tablespoons Clarified Butter (page 117)
2 pounds mixed wild mushrooms, thicker
*   stems removed and caps sliced*
*   (about 10 cups)*
2 shallots, minced
1/4 cup dry vermouth
3/4 cup chicken stock or rich mushroom stock
1/2 cup heavy cream
1 teaspoon minced fresh thyme
Salt and freshly ground pepper to taste
2 pounds fresh Potato Gnocchi (page 112)
6 tablespoons grated Parmesan cheese

An earthy pinot noir or burgundy works well with the earthiness of the wild mushrooms. Most people would not think to pair a red wine with gnocchi but fragrant and delicious wild mushrooms are complemented by pinot noir.

Special kitchen equipment
large ovenproof skillet

1 Heat the olive oil with the Clarified Butter in a large ovenproof skillet. Add the mushrooms and shallots and cook over high heat for 12 minutes or until brown, stirring occasionally. Add the vermouth and cook until the wine evaporates. Add the stock, cream and thyme. Season with salt and pepper and bring to a boil.

2 Cook the Potato Gnocchi in salted boiling water in a large saucepan until they float to the surface. Cook for 2 minutes longer; drain. Add to the mushroom mixture and cook for 1 minute, stirring constantly.

3 Stir in 4 tablespoons of the Parmesan cheese until melted. Sprinkle the remaining 2 tablespoons cheese over the top. Broil 6 inches from the heat source for 2 to 3 minutes or until golden brown and bubbly. Serve immediately.

Potato Tart

Makes 4 to 6 servings

1 Spray nonstick cooking spray over the inside and bottom of a 7 1/2-inch tart pan with a removable bottom. Place on a foil-lined baking sheet with sides.

2 Heat the olive oil in a small saucepan over medium heat. Add the shallots and reduce the heat to low. Cook for 2 minutes or until tender but not brown. Cool completely.

3 Cut the potatoes into 1/16-inch slices with a chef's knife, discarding the ends. Combine with the thyme and shallot mixture in a bowl; toss with a small rubber spatula to coat evenly.

4 Arrange an overlapping layer of potatoes in concentric circles in the prepared tart pan, starting at the outside edge. Sprinkle with kosher salt, one-fourth of the Parmigiano-Reggiano cheese and one-fourth of the Gruyère cheese. Repeat the process to make four layers.

5 Bake the tart in a preheated 400-degree oven for 45 to 50 minutes or until the top and side is golden brown, the bottom is crisp and the potatoes are tender; test for doneness with a thin cake tester.

6 Let the tart cool in the pan for 10 to 15 minutes. Loosen from the side of the pan with the pointed tip of a thin off-set metal spatula. Lift the tart from the side of the pan and loosen the tart from the bottom with the spatula. Slide the tart gently onto a cutting board and cut into four to six wedges.

Note: Starchy potatoes yield the best results in the dish. Vary the tart by using other herbs and cheeses.

3 tablespoons olive oil
1/4 cup minced shallots
   (about 2 large shallots)
1 pound unpeeled Yukon Gold
   potatoes or russet potatoes
   (about 2 large or 3 medium)
1 teaspoon (heaping) minced
   fresh thyme
Kosher salt to taste
1/2 cup finely grated
   Parmigiano-Reggiano cheese
1 cup finely grated Gruyère cheese

A fairly full-bodied wine such as a pinot blanc from California or Alsace from France is great with cheese and vegetable dishes such as this potato tart.

Special kitchen equipment
7 1/2-inch tart pan with removable bottom; chef's knife; thin offset metal spatula

Vegetable Stew in Sugar Pumpkins with Chipotle Cream Sauce

Makes 6 to 8 servings

6 to 8 medium-small sugar pumpkins
1/4 cup (1/2 stick) unsalted butter
1 yellow onion, finely chopped
4 garlic cloves, minced
2 carrots, peeled and finely chopped
2 ribs celery, finely chopped
1 pound button mushrooms, sliced
2 cups wild mushrooms, stems removed
   and caps finely chopped
2 teaspoons fresh thyme leaves
1/4 cup olive oil
2 tablespoons unsalted butter
1 cup fresh corn kernels (cut from
   about 2 ears)
1 1/2 cups chopped zucchini
   (small and young are best)
Kosher salt and freshly ground pepper to taste
Chipotle Cream Sauce (page 71)
8 to 10 sprigs cilantro, minced, for garnish
4 large purple kale leaves, for garnish

A great cold weather stew demands a well-structured but fruity wine. For this dish, a syrah works well. There are very good syrahs from California, or try shiraz from Australia or Rhône from France.

Special kitchen equipment
large roasting pan

1 Cut the pumpkin stems to a length of one inch. Cut lids from the pumpkins as for jack-o'-lanterns. Scoop out and discard the seeds and scrape off any seeds clinging to the lids. Place the pumpkins in a large roasting pan and fill each pumpkin two-thirds full with hot water. Replace the lids and add 1 inch of hot water to the roasting pan.

2 Bake in a preheated 350-degree oven for 1 hour or until the pumpkins are fork-tender but the shells hold their shape. Remove the pumpkins carefully from the pan and cool. Drain the hot water from the pumpkins and keep warm.

3 Melt 1/4 cup butter in a large saucepan over medium heat. Add the onion, garlic, carrots and celery to the saucepan. Sauté until the onions are tender-crisp. Add the mushrooms and thyme. Sauté for 15 minutes longer or until the mushrooms lose their moisture, stirring frequently.

4 Heat the olive oil and 2 tablespoons butter in a large sauté pan until hot. Add the corn and zucchini. Sauté over medium-high heat for 7 minutes or until the corn begins to brown, stirring frequently. Add to the mushroom mixture and season with kosher salt and pepper.

5 Spoon the stew into the pumpkins, filling each half full. Ladle the Chipotle Cream Sauce over the vegetable mixture and garnish with cilantro. Replace the lids and arrange on a plate lined with kale leaves. Serve immediately.

Note: Sugar pumpkins make an interesting and colorful way to serve Vegetable Stew in the fall. When sugar pumpkins are not in season, use colorful bowls keyed to the season.

Chipotle Cream Sauce

Makes about 2¹/₂ cups

Combine the chiles, stock and Crème Fraîche in a blender. Process until puréed. Combine with the sherry in a saucepan and bring to a boil. Reduce the heat and simmer for 10 minutes or until thickened, stirring frequently. Season with the kosher salt, pepper and nutmeg. Keep warm until serving time.

2 chipotle chiles in adobo sauce
3/4 cup vegetable stock
1¹/2 cups Crème Fraîche (page 116)
1 tablespoon dry sherry
1 teaspoon kosher salt
1 teaspoon freshly ground pepper
1/8 teaspoon freshly grated nutmeg

Special kitchen equipment
blender

Fabulous Finishes

Silky Chocolate Mousse

Makes 6 servings

1¹/4 cups chopped best-quality
    semisweet chocolate
¹/4 cup strong brewed coffee
4 egg yolks
2 tablespoons sugar
Pinch of kosher salt
³/4 cup milk
2 cups heavy whipping cream
¹/2 cup heavy whipping cream, for garnish
3 tablespoons shaved dark chocolate,
    for garnish

Red wine and chocolate is the ultimate indulgence. Try a hearty California cabernet with this mousse for an excellent end to dinner.

Special kitchen equipment
thermometer (optional); fine-mesh strainer

1 Combine the semisweet chocolate and coffee in a large glass microwave-safe bowl. Microwave on Medium until the chocolate begins to melt; stir the mixture.

2 Combine the egg yolks with the sugar and kosher salt in a small mixing bowl. Whisk just until blended. Heat the milk in a medium saucepan just until bubbles begin to form around the edge; do not boil. Drizzle half the milk into the egg yolk mixture, whisking constantly. Whisk the egg yolk mixture into the remaining milk in the saucepan. Cook over low heat until the custard thickens just enough to coat the back of the spoon, stirring constantly; test with a thermometer for a temperature not to exceed 160 degrees.

3 Strain the custard through a strainer into the chocolate, whisking until smooth. Remove to a large bowl and let stand until a thermometer reads 96 degrees, stirring occasionally; do not allow the mixture to set.

4 Beat 2 cups cream in a bowl until soft peaks form. Fold half the whipped cream into the chocolate mixture with a rubber spatula until no white can be seen. Fold in the remaining whipped cream gently. Spoon into six goblets or a large bowl. Chill, covered, for 3 hours to 4 days.

5 Beat ¹/2 cup cream in a bowl until soft peaks form. Garnish the mousse with the whipped cream and shaved chocolate.

Note: If the mousse has been chilled for several days, you will need to bring it nearly to room temperature and beat it until fluffy before serving.

Lemon Mousse

Juice of 3 lemons
1/2 cup sugar
Grated zest of 1 lemon
1 tablespoon unflavored gelatin
6 egg whites, at room temperature
1/2 cup sugar
3 cups heavy whipping cream,
    chilled
Fresh berries and/or
    shaved chocolate, for garnish

1 Combine the lemon juice, 1/2 cup sugar and the lemon zest in a small heatproof bowl; stir until the sugar dissolves. Sprinkle the gelatin over the mixture and let stand until softened. Place the bowl in a small shallow saucepan filled halfway with hot water. Heat until the gelatin dissolves, stirring to mix well. Cool slightly.

2 Beat the egg whites in a mixing bowl until medium-stiff peaks form. Reduce the speed and add 1/2 cup sugar gradually. Increase the speed to high and beat until the sugar is completely dissolved; test by rubbing a small amount between your thumb and finger.

3 Beat the cream in a bowl until firm peaks form. Fold the lemon mixture into the whipped cream, incorporating well. Fold the whipped cream mixture quickly into the egg whites.

4 Scoop the mousse into parfait glasses with a spring-release ice cream scoop or spoon into a large pastry bag and pipe into the parfait glasses. Cover each glass with plastic wrap and chill until serving time. Garnish with fresh berries and/or shaved chocolate to serve.

This is a perfect summer dessert. It can also be served in a glass bowl.

Special kitchen equipment
spring-action ice cream scoop or
    large pastry bag; six parfait glasses

Silky Flan

Makes 6 servings

1/2 cup superfine sugar
1/4 cup water
2 or 3 drops of lemon juice
2 eggs
3 egg yolks
1/2 cup granulated sugar
1 tablespoon light rum, coffee,
    coffee liqueur or hazelnut liqueur
2 cups milk or half-and-half
2 teaspoons vanilla extract

Special kitchen equipment
*pastry brush; six 4-ounce ramekins;
    strainer; small offset spatula*

1 Combine the superfine sugar, water and lemon juice in a medium saucepan; mix well to dissolve the sugar. Dip a pastry brush in warm water and brush down the side of the saucepan to keep the sugar from crystallizing on the saucepan. Cover with a tight-fitting lid to allow the steam to wash any undissolved sugar crystals into the liquid. Bring to a simmer and simmer until light brown; do not stir.

2 Pour the syrup immediately into six 4-ounce ramekins, tilting them to coat the sides and bottoms evenly. Invert onto a baking sheet lined with baking parchment to drain any excess.

3 Combine the eggs and egg yolks in a large bowl and whisk to mix well. Stir in the granulated sugar and rum. Bring the milk to a simmer in a medium saucepan. Stir in the vanilla. Drizzle into the egg mixture very gradually, whisking constantly. Strain into a glass measuring cup with a pouring spout. Pour equally into the prepared ramekins.

4 Place the ramekins in a baking pan lined with a kitchen towel to keep the ramekins from slipping and the bottoms from overcooking. Add enough hot water to the baking pan to reach halfway up the sides of the ramekins. Cover tightly with foil. Bake in a preheated 315-degree oven for 45 to 60 minutes or until the sides are set and the centers shake slightly.

5 Cool the flans to room temperature. Cover with plastic wrap and chill in the refrigerator; the flans will set up as they chill, but the caramel will remain liquid. Loosen the flans from the ramekins with a small offset spatula. Invert into serving dishes, allowing the caramel to run down the side of the flan and pool in the dishes.

Chile Pots de Crème

1 Combine the granulated sugar, water and lemon juice in a medium saucepan; mix well to dissolve the sugar. Dip a pastry brush in warm water and brush down the side of the saucepan to keep the sugar from crystallizing on the saucepan. Cover with a tight-fitting lid to allow the steam to wash any undissolved sugar crystals into the liquid. Bring to a simmer and cook over medium-low heat until dark golden caramel in color; do not stir. Remove from the heat.

2 Bring 1¹/2 cups cream to a simmer in a saucepan or microwave in a microwave-safe bowl until scalded. Add the caramel syrup and mix well. Cool slightly.

3 Beat the egg yolks in a saucepan until pale yellow and thick. Drizzle the cream mixture gradually into the egg yolks. Cook over low heat until the mixture coats the back of a wooden spoon, stirring constantly; do not boil. You can also use a thermometer to test for a temperature of 154 degrees. Remove from the heat and stir in the vanilla.

4 Melt the chocolate in a double boiler or in a microwave-safe bowl in the microwave. Whisk in the custard and the chimayo chile. Strain into ramekins or pots de crème dishes. Cool to room temperature. Cover with plastic wrap and chill until set.

5 Beat ¹/2 cup cream in a bowl until slightly thickened. Add the confectioners' sugar and rum and beat until medium peaks form. Spoon into a pastry bag fitted with a star tip. Pipe a rosette onto the center of each custard. Garnish with a sprinkle of baking cocoa or additional confectioners' sugar. Store, covered, in the refrigerator for up to 5 days.

Makes 6 servings

1/3 cup granulated sugar
2 tablespoons water
1 drop of lemon juice
1¹/2 cups heavy cream
6 egg yolks
1 tablespoon vanilla extract
1/2 cup chopped semisweet chocolate or dark chocolate
1 teaspoon ground chimayo chile (optional)
1/2 cup heavy whipping cream
1/2 tablespoon confectioners' sugar
1/2 tablespoon rum or brandy
Baking cocoa or confectioners' sugar, for garnish

This has always been one of our top ten favorite individual desserts. It is easy to make and packed with layers of flavor. The first taste is the deep caramel, followed by a smooth intense chocolate flavor with a zing of chile. It is sure to satisfy sophisticated chocolate lovers.

Special kitchen equipment
pastry brush; thermometer (optional); fine-mesh strainer; six ramekins or pots de crème dishes; pastry bag with a star tip

Pastry Cream

Makes 3 cups

4 egg yolks
1/2 cup milk
1/2 cup sugar
1/4 cup cornstarch
1 1/2 cups milk
2 tablespoons unsalted butter
1 teaspoon vanilla extract (optional)
1 tablespoon dark rum (optional)

To stabilize Pastry Cream, sprinkle 2 teaspoons unflavored gelatin over 1/4 cup cold water in a small glass bowl. Let stand until softened. Place the bowl in a small shallow saucepan with enough water to reach halfway up the side of the bowl. Heat until the gelatin is dissolved. Fold into the warm Pastry Cream and chill slightly. Whip 1/2 cup heavy whipping cream in a bowl until soft peaks form. Stir 1/4 of the whipped cream into the Pastry Cream, and then fold in the remaining whipped cream. Store, covered, in the refrigerator.

Special kitchen equipment
medium-mesh strainer

1 Whisk the egg yolks with 1/2 cup milk in a small bowl. Whisk the sugar and cornstarch together in a medium bowl. Add the egg yolk mixture and whisk until smooth.

2 Bring 1 1/2 cups milk to a boil in a medium saucepan over high heat; remove from the heat. Add half the hot milk to the egg yolk mixture very gradually, whisking constantly. Return the saucepan to the heat and whisk in the egg yolk mixture. Cook over medium heat for 5 to 10 minutes or until thickened and bubbly, stirring constantly to prevent scorching.

3 Remove from the heat and stir in the butter, vanilla and rum. Strain through a medium-mesh strainer into a glass bowl. Place a piece of plastic wrap directly on the surface to keep a skin from forming. Store, covered, in the refrigerator for up to 4 days.

Note: This rich custard is used as a basic building block in a number of recipes. It differs from a classic Crème Patisserie in that it is thickened with cornstarch rather than flour, giving it a silkier texture and an attractive sheen. Use Pastry Cream as the filling for fresh fruit tarts, Éclairs (page 80), Miniature Napoleons (page 85), or other desserts.

Wine-Poached Pears with Crème Anglaise

1 Mix the wine and sugar in a nonreactive saucepan. Add the orange zest, cinnamon sticks and cloves. Stand the pears in the saucepan. Cut a piece of baking parchment the size of the saucepan and place over the pears.

2 Bring to a boil and then reduce the heat to a simmer. Cook for 30 to 45 minutes or until a skewer inserted into the thicker end of a pear meets little or no resistance.

3 Remove the pears to a plate with a slotted spoon. Chill in the refrigerator. Cut the pears and stems into halves vertically and remove the cores with a melon baller. Place cut side down on a work surface and slice, cutting to but not through the stem ends. Fan the slices on serving plates and top with Crème Anglaise.

Makes 4 to 6 servings

5 cups zinfandel or other wine
1/2 cup sugar
Zest of 1 orange, cut into strips
2 cinnamon sticks, broken
4 to 6 whole cloves
4 to 6 Bosc pears, peeled and stems intact
Crème Anglaise (below)

Special kitchen equipment
baking parchment; melon baller

Crème Anglaise

1 Whisk the egg yolks in a medium bowl. Add the sugar and salt gradually, beating constantly for 2 to 3 minutes or until the mixture is pale yellow and thick enough to form a ribbon.

2 Bring the half-and-half to a simmer in a heavy medium saucepan. Cool slightly. Drizzle half the half-and-half over the egg yolk mixture in a steady stream, whisking constantly. Whisk the egg yolk mixture into the remaining half-and-half in the saucepan.

3 Place a thermometer in the sauce and place over medium-low heat. Cook for 20 to 25 minutes or until thick and smooth enough to coat the back of the spoon, stirring constantly with a wooden spoon; do not allow the temperature to rise above 170 degrees; adjust the heat if necessary to maintain the proper temperature. The longer it takes the sauce to reach the desired thickness, the creamier it will be.

4 Strain into a medium bowl and stir in the vanilla paste. Place a piece of plastic wrap directly on the surface. Chill in the refrigerator or set in a larger bowl of ice water to chill more quickly. Serve chilled or at room temperature.

Makes 2 1/2 to 3 cups

8 egg yolks
2/3 cup sugar
Pinch of salt
2 cups half-and-half
1 tablespoon vanilla paste

This is a great dessert sauce or base for ice cream. Change the flavor by infusing the hot half-and-half with strips of orange zest, toasted chopped hazelnuts, or flavored extracts. You can save the egg whites for another use by freezing them in small freezer bags and thawing in the refrigerator overnight.

Special kitchen equipment
thermometer; fine-mesh strainer

Éclairs and Cream Puffs

Pâte à Choux
3/4 cup milk
1/2 cup (1 stick) unsalted butter
1 tablespoon sugar
1/2 teaspoon salt
1 cup bread flour
2 eggs
3 or 4 egg whites

Éclairs
1 egg
1 teaspoon cold water
Apricot Glaze (see page 81)
Chocolate Glaze (see page 81)
1/2 cup smooth strawberry jam
1/2 recipe Pastry Cream (page 78)
1 cup heavy whipping cream, whipped to
  firm peaks

Pâte à choux is not really dough in the strictest sense, but dough made into a thick paste with the addition of eggs. The more eggs that can be added to the basic mixture without causing it to lose its shape when piped, the higher and lighter the finished product will be—ideally becoming a hollow shell.

Special kitchen equipment
flat-edge wooden spoon; stand mixer fitted
  with a paddle attachment; baking
  parchment; medium pastry bag with
  a medium star tip; pastry bag with a
  1/2-inch plain tip; pastry bag with a
  1/2-inch star tip

Pâte à Choux

1 Combine the milk, butter, sugar and salt in a heavy saucepan. Bring to a boil and then stir in the bread flour all at once with a flat-edge wooden spoon. Cook for 1 minute or until the mixture balls up around the spoon and pulls away from the side of the pan, stirring vigorously; the surface of the dough should have a satin sheen and the bottom of the saucepan should have a thin film.

2 Remove to a stand mixer fitted with a paddle attachment and cool slightly. Add the eggs one at a time, mixing well after each addition. Beat in three of the egg whites one at a time. Check the consistency of the dough at this point. When the paddle is lifted up, some of the dough should be firm enough to be pulled up with the paddle; it should then detach into a peak that slowly bends over. You can omit or add the fourth egg to achieve the correct consistency.

Notes: Cool the dough slightly before adding the eggs. Add only as many eggs as will allow the dough to hold its firm consistency. Stop mixing when there is still one egg white to add and check to see if some of the dough will lift up and detach to form a slowly bending peak. You may not need the last egg white.

Work with the dough while it is still warm, as it cannot be handled when it cools.

Éclairs

3 Cut a piece of baking parchment to fit a baking sheet. Mark 3-inch lengths on the paper, leaving space between the marks for the pastry to expand; allow for no more than twenty éclairs on each baking sheet. Place the baking parchment with the marked side down on a baking sheet.

4 Place the warm dough in a medium pastry bag fitted with a medium star tip. Press the dough toward the tip end with the flat edge of a large spatula or plastic dough scraper to expel excess air. Twist the bag for better control and pipe the dough onto the marked paper. Brush with a wash of the egg beaten with the cold water, taking care that the wash does not run down the sides to stick the dough to the paper and prevent rising.

5 Place in a preheated 300-degree oven and then increase the temperature to 410 degrees. Bake for 25 minutes or until the éclairs are golden brown and puffed to three times their uncooked size. Press the tops gently with a fork dipped in cool water to level. Brush again with the egg wash.

6 Cut off the top third of each éclair and remove to a work surface. Brush the tops with Apricot Glaze and let stand until set. Place a bowl with Chocolate Glaze in a larger bowl of warm water. Let stand until the glaze has a thin consistency. Dip the éclair tops in the chocolate. Let stand until set.

7 Spoon the strawberry jam into a pastry bag fitted with a 1/2-inch plain tip. Pipe a small ribbon of jam into the bottom of each éclair. Whisk the Pastry Cream in a bowl and then fold in the whipped cream. Spoon the Pastry Cream into a pastry bag fitted with a 1/2-inch star tip. Pipe a coil of cream on top of the jam, making it 1/2 inch higher than the top of the éclair. Replace the tops of the éclairs at a slight angle to allow the filling to show. Serve as soon as possible.

Note: Unfilled baked pastries can be well wrapped and frozen for several weeks

Cream Puffs

8 Scoop the warm dough onto the baking parchment-lined baking sheets and brush each with the egg wash. Place in the lower half of a preheated 300-degree oven and then increase the temperature to 410 degrees. Bake for 25 to 30 minutes. Decrease the oven temperature to 300 degrees and bake for 15 to 20 minutes longer or until golden brown. Remove to a wire rack and let stand until cool enough to handle. Pierce a hole in each to allow the steam to escape. Fill and glaze as above.

Note: Beginning with a lower temperature and increasing the heat once you place the baking sheet in the oven will result in a lighter and higher finished product. Reducing the heat after the puffs are well risen allows them to dry without burning.

Make **Apricot Glaze** by bringing 4 ounces apricot preserves to a boil in a 1-quart saucepan. Remove from the heat and stir in 1 tablespoon brandy. Strain through a medium-mesh strainer and cool slightly.

Prepare **Chocolate Glaze** by placing 4 ounces dark chocolate in a 1-quart microwave-safe bowl. Microwave on High at 20-second intervals until completely melted, stirring with a silicone spatula. Stir in 1 tablespoon corn syrup.

Use bread flour for higher, lighter puffs. The milk mixture must be heated to a full bubbling boil and the butter completely melted before adding the flour. Cook the mixture for about 1 minute longer after adding the flour to remove the raw taste of the flour and allow it to absorb the needed number of eggs.

81

Wine-Poached Peach Tartlets

Makes 6 servings

Juice and zest strips of 1 small orange
3 to 4 cups white zinfandel
1/4 cup sugar
6 whole cloves
2 cinnamon sticks, broken
3 yellow peaches or pears, peeled,
*   or 6 canned peach halves in light syrup*
6 sheets Classic Puff Pastry
*   (page 118), chilled*
2 teaspoons unflavored gelatin
1/2 cup heavy whipping cream
1/2 recipe Pastry Cream (page 78)
2 tablespoons peach brandy
1/4 cup Caramel Cream (page 92)

You will agree that the finished tartlets are worth the extra effort needed to assemble the several components of this dish. If you are using frozen puff pastry, thaw it in the refrigerator for up to 6 hours before using. You can substitute pears for the peaches in this recipe if you prefer.

Special kitchen equipment

pastry bag with a medium round tip; baking parchment; small offset spatula

1 Combine the orange juice, orange zest, 3 cups wine, the sugar, cloves and cinnamon sticks in a 6-quart saucepan. Cut a slice from the bottom of each peach so it will sit upright in the saucepan. Arrange the peaches in the saucepan and add additional wine to cover if needed. Place a circle of baking parchment over the peaches and place a small heavy lid on the paper to keep the peaches submerged.

2 Bring to a boil and then reduce the heat to a simmer. Cook for 10 minutes. Test for tenderness with a sharp cake tester; the tester should penetrate the peaches with little resistance. Do not overcook.

3 Use a slotted spoon to remove the peaches to a baking dish lined with baking parchment paper. Reserve 1/2 cup of the poaching liquid; discard the remaining liquid. Let the peaches stand until cool enough to handle. Cut each peach into halves vertically, discarding the pits. Cover with plastic wrap and chill the peaches and poaching liquid separately for up to 2 days.

4 Make a peach-shaped template from stiff cardboard or heavy plastic and cover the template with plastic wrap. Unroll the puff pastry on a work surface and place the template on the pastry. Cut out six shapes with a sharp knife. Make slanted 1/4-inch cuts around the outer edges of the cutouts with the knife, cutting from the inside to the edge; this will allow the outer edge to puff up higher than the center.

5 Remove the cutouts to a baking parchment-lined baking sheet with a small offset spatula. Prick the centers of the cutouts with a fork. Chill for 30 minutes.

6 Place a piece of baking parchment on top of the cutouts and place a baking sheet over that. Bake in a preheated 410-degree oven for 15 minutes. Remove the top baking sheet and baking parchment. Reduce the oven temperature to 375 degrees. Bake the pastries for 30 minutes longer or until golden brown. Remove to a wire rack to cool.

7 Sprinkle the gelatin over the reserved 1/2 cup poaching liquid in a small heatproof bowl. Let stand for 3 to 4 minutes to soften. Place the bowl in a small saucepan and add enough water to reach halfway up the side. Heat just until the gelatin dissolves.

8 Beat the whipping cream in a bowl until soft peaks form. Stir 2 tablespoons of the whipped cream into the Pastry Cream; fold the Pastry Cream into the whipped cream. Stir in the peach brandy. Spoon into a pastry bag fitted with a medium round tip. Pipe a thin layer of the cream over the puff pastries.

9 Slice each peach half crosswise, cutting to but not through one side; fan out the slices slightly. Place on the prepared pastries. Brush the gelatin mixture over the peaches. Drizzle the Caramel Cream onto six serving plates. Place a peach tartlet on each plate and serve immediately.

Caramel Pumpkin Tart

Makes 12 servings

1/2 recipe European Short Pastry
*   dough (below)*
2 eggs, at room temperature
3 egg yolks, at room temperature
1 teaspoon vanilla extract
1/3 cup granulated sugar
3/4 teaspoon cinnamon
1/3 teaspoon ginger
Pinch of ground cloves
1/4 teaspoon kosher salt
1 cup heavy cream
1 1/2 cups pumpkin purée
*   (not pumpkin pie filling)*
Caramel Cream (page 92)
1 cup heavy whipping cream
1 1/2 tablespoons confectioners' sugar

Special kitchen equipment
11-inch tart pan with removable bottom;
*   pastry bag with small rosette tip (optional)*

1 Spray an 11-inch tart pan with a removable bottom with butter-flavor nonstick cooking spray. Roll the European Short Pastry dough into a circle and fit it into the pan.

2 Combine the eggs, egg yolks and vanilla in a large mixing bowl and beat lightly. Add the granulated sugar, cinnamon, ginger, cloves, kosher salt and 1 cup heavy cream and stir to mix well; do not beat. Stir in the pumpkin purée. Strain into a large bowl and add 1/4 cup of the Caramel Cream. Spoon into the prepared tart pan.

3 Bake in a preheated 375-degree oven for 1 hour or until the tip of a paring knife inserted into the center comes out clean; do not shake the tart while it is baking. Cool on a wire rack. Chill, uncovered, in the refrigerator for up to 3 days.

4 Drizzle the remaining Caramel Cream onto serving plates. Whip 1 cup heavy cream with the confectioners' sugar in a mixing bowl until firm peaks form. Spoon into a pastry bag fitted with a small rosette tip. Pipe into rosettes around the tart of place a dollop of whipped cream on each serving. Place on the prepared plates.

Note: The basic pumpkin filling for this tart was inspired by my friend and pastry chef, Aimee Altizer.

European Short Pastry

Makes two 11-inch tart shells

1/2 cup (scant) sugar
14 tablespoons unsalted butter, softened
1/2 egg, beaten
1/2 teaspoon vanilla extract
1 2/3 cups bread flour

Special kitchen equipment
stand mixer fitted with a dough hook;
*   two 11-inch tart pans with removable*
*   bottoms; baking parchment; pie weights*
*   or dried beans*

1 Spray two 11-inch tart pans with removable bottoms with nonstick baking spray. Combine the sugar, butter, egg and vanilla in the bowl of a stand mixer fitted with a dough hook. Beat at low speed until mixed. Add the bread flour and mix just until a smooth dough is formed. Divide into two portions.

2 Press each pastry portion between two sheets of plastic wrap on a work surface to flatten. Roll into circles 1/8 inch thick. Place on a rimless baking sheet and chill for 10 to 15 minutes.

3 Remove the top sheet of plastic wrap from each pastry circle and use the edges of the bottom sheet of plastic to invert into the prepared tart pans. Trim the top edges and prick the bottoms and sides of the pastries with a fork. Chill in the refrigerator for 10 to 15 minutes.

4 Cut circles of baking parchment 1 inch larger than the tart pans. Spray the paper lightly with nonstick baking spray. Place the circles on the pastry shells and fill with pie weights or dried beans, covering the bottoms and part of the way up the sides.

5 Bake in a preheated 350-degree oven for 15 minutes. Lift out the baking parchment and pie weights carefully. Press the pastry lightly to repair any tears. Bake for 10 minutes longer or until light golden brown. Fill as desired while till hot.

You may also fill the pastry before baking. Mix the dough lightly, as it becomes harder to roll when it is overmixed.

Miniature Napoleons

1 Roll the Puff Pastry to a thin rectangle $1/8$ inch thick on a work surface. Roll the dough around the rolling pin and unroll it onto a baking sheet lined with baking parchment. Chill for 15 minutes.

2 Prick the dough all over with a fork and place a sheet of baking parchment on the top. Weight with a large wire rack. Bake in a preheated 410-degree oven for 15 to 20 minutes or until it begins to brown. Remove the baking parchment and wire rack and bake for 10 minutes longer or until golden brown on both sides.

3 Slide the pastry carefully onto a cutting board. Trim the edges of the warm pastry with a chef's knife, reserving the trimmings. Cut the rectangle into $11/2 \times 3$-inch strips. Remove to the wire rack to cool completely. (Crush the trimmings to fine crumbs with a rolling pin and reserve for another use.)

4 Place a pastry strip on a work surface and spread evenly with a small amount of the Pastry Cream. Add a second pastry strip and spread with cream. Top with a third strip and press lightly. Repeat with the remaining pastry strips and Pastry Cream. Sift the confectioners' sugar over the pastries. Garnish with fresh fruit.

Makes 24 small napoleons

*1 recipe Classic Puff Pastry (page 118)
   or 1 package thawed frozen puff
   pastry, chilled
2 cups Pastry Cream (page 78)
1/2 cup confectioners' sugar
Fresh fruit, for garnish*

The parts for this delicacy can be prepared in advance, but should be assembled no more than 2 hours before serving. Napoleons make a satisfying ending to a meal or a special treat with afternoon tea.

Special kitchen equipment
*baking parchment; wire rack; chef's
   knife; offset spatula*

Asian Pear Tarte Tatin

Makes 4 servings

4 Asian pears, peeled and cored
3/4 cup sugar
1/4 cup water
1/4 cup (1/2 stick) unsalted butter, melted
2 ounces almond paste (optional)
1/4 cup minced pistachios (optional)
8 ounces Classic Puff Pastry (page 118) or
   frozen puff pastry, thawed
Crème Fraîche (page 116) or chopped
   pistachios, for garnish

The cooled pears can be reheated at 375 degrees for several minutes. The reserved caramel sauce can be reheated in a microwave or small saucepan.

Special kitchen equipment
vegetable peeler; pastry brush; four 6-ounce ramekins; 3 1/2-inch round cookie cutter

1 Place the pears into four 6-ounce ramekins to see if they will fit. Pare lightly with a vegetable peeler or paring knife if necessary to fit; remove the pears.

2 Combine the sugar and water in a medium saucepan, stirring to mix well. Cook over medium heat for 7 to 8 minutes or until the sugar dissolves, stirring constantly. Dip a pastry brush into warm water and wash down the side of the saucepan to remove any undissolved sugar crystals. Cover the saucepan and cook until the mixture caramelizes to a light amber color. Pour evenly into the ramekins.

3 Brush the pears all over with some of the melted butter and place in the prepared ramekins. Mix the almond paste and pistachios in a small bowl. Spoon into the centers of the pears and place the ramekins on a baking sheet. Bake in a preheated 375-degree oven for 30 minutes.

4 Roll the Puff Pastry 1/4 inch thick on a lightly floured work surface. Prick the pastry all over with a fork. Cut four circles 3 1/2 inches in diameter with a cookie cutter or use a ramekin and small sharp knife to cut circles large enough to cover the tops of the ramekins.

5 Remove the baking sheet with the ramekins carefully from the oven. Brush the exposed surfaces of the pears with the remaining melted butter. Place one pastry circle on top of each pear and press around the pear, taking care, as the pears will be very hot. Bake for 35 to 40 minutes longer or until the pears are tender when tested with a thin cake tester and the pastry is brown, rotating the pan during the baking time.

6 Place a wire rack over a shallow baking pan. Cool the tarts in the ramekins on the wire rack for several minutes. Flip each tart carefully onto the rack with a spatula; some of the caramel sauce will drain into the baking pan. Pour the caramel sauce into a small bowl and reserve.

7 Cool for 5 minutes. Brush the exposed surface of the pears with the reserved caramel sauce. Serve warm, garnished with a swirl of Crème Fraîche or a sprinkle of chopped pistachios.

Perfect Bread Pudding

Makes 8 servings

1/4 cup golden raisins (optional)
2 tablespoons rum
2 cups milk
1/2 cup light cream
Grated zest of 1/2 orange
Grated zest of 1/2 lemon
6 cups (1/2-inch cubes) day-old bread
2 eggs
2 egg yolks
1/2 cup sugar
1 teaspoon vanilla extract
Pinch of salt

Special kitchen equipment
thermometer (optional)

1 Combine the raisins with the rum in a medium glass bowl and let stand to soak. Combine the milk, cream, orange zest and lemon zest in a saucepan. Bring to a simmer over medium heat; remove from the heat and cover. Let steep for 1 hour.

2 Scatter half the bread cubes loosely in a 1 1/2-quart baking dish. Drain the raisins, reserving the rum. Sprinkle the raisins over the bread and top with the remaining bread cubes.

3 Beat the eggs and egg yolks lightly in a large bowl. Add the milk mixture, sugar, vanilla and salt gradually, mixing constantly. Stir in the reserved rum. Pour evenly over the bread in the baking dish. Let stand for 1 hour or longer, pressing down occasionally with a spatula to allow the bread to absorb the liquid.

4 Place the baking dish in a larger pan with sides deeper that the baking dish. Add enough hot water to reach 1 inch up the sides of the baking dish. Bake in a preheated 325-degree oven for 40 to 45 minutes or until a skewer inserted in the center comes out almost clean; you can test for an appropriate internal temperature of 130 degrees with a thermometer. Broil for several minutes to brown if desired. Serve at room temperature with Crème Anglaise (page 79) or Caramel Cream (page 92). Store leftovers, tightly covered, in the refrigerator for up to 5 days.

Notes: Bread pudding is the perfect way to use leftover croissants or brioche. You can save bread in the freezer until you have enough for the recipe. Perfect bread pudding is moist without being soupy. The bread should be loose when it is soaking, with some liquid visible around the edges. Too much bread will cause the pudding to be dense and dry. Bread pudding that is overcooked will be tough and rubbery and may separate, leaving a puddle of liquid in the dish. To avoid overcooking, test for doneness by gently jiggling the pan; it should shimmy. Bread pudding should never rise in the oven.

Strawberry Gelée and Basil Panna Cotta

Strawberry Gelée

1 Combine 18 ounces strawberries and 1/4 cup superfine sugar in a double boiler or stainless steel bowl. Cover with plastic wrap and place over simmering water. Cook over low heat for 45 minutes or until the strawberries have released their juices. Pour through a colander over a bowl to catch the juices. Place the colander and bowl in the refrigerator and allow to drain for 5 to 6 hours or until well chilled.

2 Pour the strained juice into a small heatproof bowl; juice should measure about 3/4 cup. Discard the strawberries. Sprinkle the gelatin over the juice and let stand for 2 minutes or until softened. Heat the water in a small skillet and place the glass bowl in the water. Heat until the gelatin dissolves, stirring to blend well.

3 Process 6 ounces strawberries in a blender until puréed. Combine with the lemon juice and 2 tablespoons sugar in a bowl and mix well. Stir in the gelatin mixture. Let stand for 1 hour or until the mixture has the consistency of unbeaten egg whites; place in an ice water bath to speed the process if desired. Pour into six parfait glasses. Chill until set.

Basil Panna Cotta

5 Heat the cream in a medium saucepan until steaming. Add the sugar, stirring to dissolve it completely. Remove from the heat and stir in the basil. Cover tightly and let stand for 20 minutes. Strain into a bowl.

6 Sprinkle the gelatin over the cold water in a small heatproof bowl. Let stand for 2 to 3 minutes to soften. Place in a small skillet with enough water to reach halfway up the side of the bowl. Heat just until the gelatin dissolves, stirring to mix well. Add to the cream mixture. Chill until set.

7 Spoon the panna cotta evenly over the strawberry gelée in the parfait glasses. Chill until completely set or for up to 4 days. Cut three fresh strawberries into halves lengthwise. Slice into fans, cutting to but not through the stem ends. Place one fan on each parfait and add a fresh basil leaf to each. Serve immediately.

Makes 6 servings

Strawberry Gelée
18 ounces fresh strawberries, cut into 3/4-inch pieces (about 3 1/3 cups)
1/4 cup superfine sugar
1 teaspoon unflavored gelatin
1 cup water
6 ounces fresh strawberries
2 teaspoons fresh lemon juice
2 tablespoons superfine sugar

Basil Panna Cotta
2 cups heavy cream
6 tablespoons granulated sugar
2 tablespoons chopped fresh basil
2 teaspoons unflavored gelatin
3 tablespoons cold water
3 fresh strawberries, for garnish
6 basil leaves, for garnish

Every summer, this is a favorite dessert for adults and kids alike. For kids, substitute mint leaves for the basil.

Special kitchen equipment
colander; blender; six parfait glasses

Dutch Apple Strudel

Apple Filling

2 Fuji apples, or other baking apples
1/4 cup packed light or dark brown sugar
3 tablespoons granulated sugar
1 teaspoon fresh lemon juice
3/4 teaspoon cinnamon
Pinch of freshly grated nutmeg
1/4 teaspoon kosher salt
3 tablespoons unsalted butter
1 teaspoon vanilla extract

Strudel

2 sheets frozen puff pastry, thawed in the
   refrigerator overnight
1 egg, beaten
1 tablespoon water
1/4 cup cake crumbs or cookie
   crumbs (optional)
1 teaspoon coarse sugar or fine granulated
   sugar (optional)

Precooking the apples reduces their juices and keeps the bottom crust from becoming soggy. You can prepare the filling up to two days in advance and store it in a covered container in the refrigerator.

Special kitchen equipment

*heatproof rubber spatula; pastry brush;
   baking parchment; long offset spatula*

Filling

1 Peel and core the apples. Cut each into halves and then slice crosswise into 1/2-inch slices. Combine the apples with the brown sugar, granulated sugar, lemon juice, cinnamon, nutmeg and kosher salt in a large bowl; toss to coat evenly. Melt the butter in a 12-inch skillet over medium heat. Cook for 1 to 2 minutes or until the milk solids are golden brown. Remove from the heat and stir in the vanilla.

2 Add the apple mixture carefully to the skillet, scraping the sugar and spices from the bowl into the skillet with a heatproof rubber spatula. Stir to coat well with the butter and spread in an even layer.

3 Cook over medium heat for 10 to 13 minutes or until the apples are tender but still hold their shape, stirring gently with the spatula every few minutes; try not to break up the apples. Spoon onto a shallow baking sheet and let stand until cool.

Strudel

4 Unfold one sheet of the puff pastry on a floured work surface, gently pinching together any seams that have split. Roll the dough into a 12×14-inch rectangle. Cut into halves lengthwise with a sharp knife to form two 6×14-inch rectangles. Remove one of the rectangles to a baking parchment-lined baking sheet.

5 Beat the egg with the water in a cup. Brush the egg wash around the edges of the dough with a pastry brush, taking care that the wash does not run down the edges. Sprinkle with the cake crumbs to absorb the filling juices. Spoon half the apple mixture in a 4-inch wide strip down the length of the rectangle; drizzle with any remaining juices.

6 Dust the remaining puff pastry half with flour and gently fold in half lengthwise; do not press the fold. Cut 1 1/2-inch slashes at 1-inch intervals along the folded side of the pastry, leaving a 1-inch border around the remaining edges.

7 Lift the folded pastry with a long offset spatula and place over the filled pastry. Unfold the top pastry gently and press the edges to seal. Crimp the edges gently with a fork. Repeat the process with the remaining pastry and filling. Chill for 15 to 20 minutes. Brush the tops with the remaining egg wash and sprinkle with the sugar

8 Place on a rack in the lower third of a preheated 400-degree oven. Bake the strudels for 15 minutes. Rotate the baking sheet and bake until the pastry is puffed, deep golden brown on the top and light golden brown on the bottom; lift the bottom with a spatula to check.

9 Cool the strudels on the baking sheet for several minutes. Remove with the baking parchment to a wire rack to cool slightly. Serve warm with sweetened whipped cream. Store, wrapped in foil, in the refrigerator for up to 3 days. Reheat at 325 degrees for 5 minutes.

Pumpkin Ginger Cheesecake

Gingersnap Crust
2 ounces gingersnaps, crushed
1/3 cup almond meal
2 tablespoons unsalted butter, melted

Cheesecake
1 cup pumpkin purée (not pumpkin
pie filling)
32 ounces cream cheese, softened
1 1/2 cups sugar
2/3 cup sour cream
2 tablespoons molasses
Splash of rum or bourbon
2 teaspoons cinnamon
2 teaspoons ginger
Dash of allspice
Dash of ground cloves
Dash of freshly ground nutmeg
4 eggs, beaten
Sweetened whipped cream, for garnish

Special kitchen equipment
food processor; 10-inch springform pan; large
spring-action ice cream scoop (optional)

Crust

1 Combine the cookie crumbs, almond meal and butter in a food processor and pulse until well mixed. Press over the bottom of a 10-inch springform pan sprayed with butter-flavor nonstick cooking spray.

Cheesecake

2 Combine the pumpkin purée, cream cheese, sugar, sour cream, molasses, rum, cinnamon, ginger, allspice, cloves and nutmeg in a food processor. Pulse until well blended. Scrape down the side of the food processor and pulse for 30 seconds. Add the eggs and pulse for 30 seconds longer.

3 Scoop the mixture into the springform pan with a large spring-action ice cream scoop. Bake in a preheated 280-degree oven for 1 hour or just until the center shakes slightly; do not overbake. Cool in the pan on a wire rack. Chill in the refrigerator for up to 24 hours. Place on a serving plate. Loosen the cheesecake from the side of the pan with a spatula and remove the side of the pan. Serve chilled, garnished with a dollop of whipped cream.

Note: For those of us that are passionate about pumpkin, this is the dessert for you. It's always smooth, with just the right amount of spices. It's a must for the holidays.

Caramel Cream

1/4 cup water
2 drops of lemon juice
1/2 cup sugar
1/4 cup heavy cream, heated

Special kitchen equipment
pastry brush

1 Combine the water, lemon juice and sugar in a medium saucepan and stir to dissolve the sugar. Dip a pastry brush into water and brush down the side of the saucepan to remove any undissolved sugar crystals.

2 Cover the saucepan tightly and cook over medium heat until golden brown, lifting the lid occasionally to check the color. Remove from the heat and stir in the cream carefully. Cool slightly. Serve with the Caramel Pumpkin Tart (page 84) or other desserts.

Carrot Cake

Cake

1 Combine the raisins with just enough hot water to cover in a glass bowl. Stir in 1 tablespoon rum and let stand at room temperature for 1 hour or in the refrigerator for up to 2 weeks; drain.

2 Mix the flour, baking powder, baking soda, baking cocoa and cinnamon together. Combine the granulated sugar, brown sugar, canola oil, eggs, molasses, 2 tablespoons rum and the vanilla in a stand mixer; mix until smooth. Add the dry ingredients and beat at low speed just until moistened. Fold in the carrots, walnuts, pecans and raisins.

3 Spoon the batter into two 8-inch cake pans sprayed with nonstick baking spray. Bake in a preheated 350-degree oven for 40 to 45 minutes or until the centers are firm and the layers pull from the edges of the pans; do not overbake.

4 Cool in the pans on a wire rack for 5 minutes. Remove the cake layers to the wire rack to cool completely.

Frosting

5 Cream the cream cheese and butter in a food processor until smooth. Add the orange juice concentrate and pulse two or three times to blend well. Add the confectioners' sugar and pulse just until mixed; overmixing may make the frosting too thin to set up properly. Spread between the layers and over the top and side of the cake. Store in the refrigerator.

Variation: You can bake the cake in a 9×13-inch cake pan if preferred and cut into bars. There may be more frosting than needed for this size cake.

Makes 12 servings

Cake
1 cup golden raisins
1 tablespoon rum
2 cups all-purpose flour
3/4 teaspoon baking powder
3/4 teaspoon baking soda
2 teaspoons baking cocoa
2 teaspoons cinnamon
1 cup granulated sugar
1 cup packed brown sugar
1 1/4 cups canola oil
4 eggs, at room temperature
2 tablespoons mild-flavored molasses
2 tablespoons rum
1 teaspoon vanilla extract
2 cups shredded carrots
    (about 6 carrots)
1 cup walnut pieces
1 cup pecan pieces, toasted

Orange Cream Cheese Frosting
12 ounces cream cheese, softened
6 tablespoons unsalted butter, softened
2 tablespoons frozen orange juice
    concentrate, at room temperature
3/4 cup confectioners' sugar, sifted

This recipe was formulated for high-altitude baking. To prepare it at low altitude, increase the baking powder and baking soda to 1 1/2 teaspoons each and the baking time may be a few minutes less. This was one of the most popular cakes in my Utopia Bakery. It is moist and keeps well in the refrigerator.

Special kitchen equipment
stand mixer; food processor

Pineapple Mango Upside-Down Cake

Makes 9 servings

2 tablespoons unsalted butter, softened
1/2 cup packed light brown sugar
1 (8-ounce) can pineapple rings, drained
1/2 cup minced fresh mango
1 (8-ounce) can crushed pineapple, drained
1 1/2 cups all-purpose flour
1/8 teaspoon baking powder
1/8 teaspoon baking soda
1/2 teaspoon salt
1/2 cup (1 stick) butter, softened
1 cup granulated sugar
2 eggs, at room temperature
1 teaspoon vanilla extract
1/4 cup Crème Fraîche (page 116) or
    sour cream

This recipe was forumlated for high-altitude baking. To prepare it at low altitude, increase the baking powder and baking soda to 1/4 teaspoon each.

Special kitchen equipment
*stand mixer fitted with a paddle attachment;
    small offset spatula*

1 Beat 2 tablespoons butter with the brown sugar in a stand mixer fitted with a paddle attachment for 2 to 3 minutes or until light and fluffy. Spread in the bottom of an 8×8-inch cake pan sprayed with nonstick baking spray.

2 Arrange the pineapple rings in the prepared pan and sprinkle some of the mango in the center of each pineapple ring. Mix the remaining mango with the crushed pineapple in a bowl and spread over the pineapple rings.

3 Sift the flour, baking powder, baking soda and salt together. Beat 1/2 cup butter and the granulated sugar in a stand mixer fitted with a paddle attachment at medium speed for 2 to 3 minutes or until light and fluffy. Beat in the eggs one at a time, scraping the side of the bowl as needed. Beat in the vanilla. Add half the flour mixture, the crème fraîche and the remaining flour mixture, mixing well after each addition.

4 Spread the batter evenly over the fruit in the prepared pan with a small offset spatula, filling the spaces. Bake in a preheated 350-degree oven for 50 minutes or until the cake is light brown and a cake tester inserted in the center comes out clean; rotate the pan halfway through the baking time. Cool in the pan on a wire rack for 30 minutes. Invert onto a cake plate and remove the baking parchment. Serve warm or at room temperature.

Note: Make this a day in advance if desired and store loosely covered at room temperature. Reheat at 300 degrees on a baking parchment-lined baking sheet for 15 minutes to serve.

Chocolate-Glazed Perfect Chocolate Cake

Cake

1 Spray two 8-inch cake pans with nonstick baking spray; line the bottoms with circles of baking parchment.

2 Pour the boiling water over the baking cocoa in a medium heatproof bowl; whisk until smooth. Cool completely. Sift the flour, baking soda, baking powder and salt together.

3 Cream the butter in a stand mixer for 30 seconds or until light. Beat in the sugar gradually; mix at medium speed for 4 1/2 minutes or until fluffy. Reduce the mixer speed to low and beat in the eggs one at a time. Add the dry ingredients alternately with the cocoa mixture, beginning and ending with the dry ingredients and mixing just until moistened after each addition. Mix in the rum and vanilla.

4 Spoon into the prepared cake pans; tap the pans gently on the counter to remove any air pockets. Place the pans on flat baking sheets and bake in a preheated 350-degree oven for 50 minutes or until the cakes pull from the edges of the pans. You can test for doneness by placing a thermometer in the center of one layer at an angle near the outer edge; the internal temperature should be 196 degrees. Do not test until the cake is set to prevent deflating.

5 Cool in the pans on a wire rack for 5 minutes. Remove from the pans and place right side up on the rack to cool completely. Remove the baking parchment and cut each layer of the cooled cake into halves horizontally. Fill with Lemon Curd or Pastry Cream. Chill in the refrigerator. Place on a rack over a baking sheet to catch the glaze.

Glaze

6 Place the chocolate in a 2-quart microwave-safe bowl. Microwave at 20-second intervals until the chocolate is smooth but not completely melted; the internal temperature should read 104 to 108 degrees on a thermometer. Stir briskly with a wooden spoon until the temperature is about 90 degrees. Stir in the Clarified Butter.

7 Ladle the glaze slowly over the center of the cake and spread with a large flat offset spatula to smoothly cover the top and side of the cake. Scrape up any excess glaze to reuse. It can be whipped with a small amount of heavy cream as a cake filling or added to Double-Chocolate Brownies (page 98) before baking.

Makes 12 servings

Cake
2 cups boiling water
1 cup Dutch-process baking cocoa
2 2/3 cups all-purpose flour
1 teaspoon baking soda
1/4 teaspoon baking powder
1/2 teaspoon salt
1 cup (2 sticks) butter, softened
2 1/2 cups sugar
4 eggs, at room temperature
1/4 cup dark rum or brandy
1 1/2 teaspoons vanilla extract
Lemon Curd (page 120), Pastry Cream (page 78) or Easy Dark Chocolate Filling (page 121), for filling

Chocolate Glaze
10 1/2 ounces European bittersweet chocolate
3 tablespoons Clarified Butter (page 117), at room temperature

This has been the favorite cake for the classes at Park City Cooking School. The students say that it is easy to make, always moist, never fails, and has a great chocolate flavor. The recipe also makes twenty-four cupcakes.

Special kitchen equipment
stand mixer; thermometer (optional); baking parchment; large flat offset spatula

New Year's Eve Clock Cake

Makes 12 servings

1 Chocolate-Glazed Perfect Chocolate Cake
(page 95)
8 ounces marzipan
Gel cake color for numbers
26 inches fancy ribbon

The cake can be prepared and stored for up to two days before decorating for this impressive presentation.

Special kitchen equipment
small metal or plastic cookie cutters in the forms of numbers (look in a cake supply store); small new artist's brush

1 Chill the Chocolate-Glazed Perfect Chocolate Cake for 30 minutes.

2 Place the marzipan on a work surface between two sheets of plastic wrap. Roll to a circle 9 inches in diameter and 1/4 inch thick. Trim to a circle 8 inches in diameter and replace the top piece of plastic wrap.

3 Gather up the scraps of marzipan. Dip a wooden pick into the cake color and mix into the marzipan scraps to achieve the desired color for the clock numbers. Roll the marzipan 1/4 inch thick on a work surface. Cut out the clock hands with a knife. Cut the numbers for the face of a clock with number cookie cutters; keep the numbers and clock hands covered with plastic wrap. I use only the numbers 3, 6, 9 and 12.

4 Remove the cake from the refrigerator and place on a cake plate or cake board. Press the ribbon around the lower edge of the cake, overlapping the ends. Remove one sheet of plastic wrap from the marzipan circle and invert directly onto the top of the cake. Press gently to stabilize and remove the second piece of plastic wrap.

5 Dip a clean artist's brush in water and brush the underside of the marzipan numbers and clock hands. Place on the cake as for the face of a clock. Press gently to stabilize. Place the cake in an airtight container or wrap loosely in plastic wrap. Chill for up to 4 days. Serve at room temperature.

Double-Chocolate Brownies

Makes 20 to 30 bars

8 ounces bittersweet chocolate

3/4 cup (1 1/2 sticks) unsalted butter, softened

4 eggs, at room temperature

1 tablespoon instant coffee granules
    (optional)

1/2 teaspoon salt

1 1/3 cups superfine sugar

1 teaspoon vanilla extract

1 cup all-purpose flour

1 1/2 cups pecan pieces

3/4 cup semisweet or dark chocolate pieces

It is said that brownies are the national sweet. These are fudgy brownies that melt in your mouth. They were the biggest seller at my Utopia Bakery and Two Coffee House in the Avenues.

Special kitchen equipment

*baking parchment; silicone spatula; stand
    mixer fitted with a paddle attachment*

1 Line a 9×14-inch baking pan with baking parchment and then spray with nonstick baking spray. Combine the bittersweet chocolate and butter in a large microwave-safe bowl. Microwave on High for 1 minute; stir with a silicone spatula. Microwave at 30-second intervals until completely melted, stirring after each interval; do not overheat.

2 Combine the eggs, coffee granules and salt in a stand mixer fitted with a paddle attachment; beat for 30 seconds. Add the sugar gradually, beating at medium speed for 30 seconds; do not overbeat. Add the chocolate mixture and vanilla; beat at low speed just until mixed. Beat in the flour just until moistened. Fold in the pecans and chocolate pieces.

3 Spread in the prepared baking pan. Bake in a preheated 350-degree oven for 35 minutes. Cool in the pan on a cooling rack. Chill for 1 hour before cutting into bars. Store the brownies in a airtight container in the refrigerator and allow to stand at room temperature for 15 to 20 minutes before serving. You may also individually wrap the brownies in plastic wrap and store in the refrigerator.

Lemon Bars Deluxe

Crust

1 Spray a 9×14-inch baking pan with nonstick baking spray and line the bottom with baking parchment. Mix the flour, lemon zest and salt together. Cream the butter and sugar in a stand mixer for 5 minutes or until light and fluffy. Add the dry ingredients and mix at low speed just until combined.

2 Press over the bottom and part of the way up the sides of the prepared pan. Chill for 30 minutes. Bake in a preheated 350-degree oven for 20 to 25 minutes or until light brown. Cool slightly.

Filling

3 Whisk the granulated sugar and flour together in bowl. Combine the eggs, lemon juice and lemon zest in a bowl; whisk until smooth. Add the sugar mixture and mix well.

4 Spread over the cooled crust. Bake for 25 to 30 minutes or just until set but slightly soft in the center; overbaking will cause the filling to crack. Cool to room temperature. Chill for 20 minutes before cutting into bars. Sprinkle with the confectioners' sugar just before serving. Store, covered, in the refrigerator for up to 6 days.

Shortbread Crust
3 1/2 cups all-purpose flour
1 teaspoon grated lemon zest
1/4 teaspoon salt
1 1/2 cups (3 sticks) unsalted
     butter, softened
3/4 cup sugar

Filling
3 1/2 cups granulated sugar
1 1/4 cups all-purpose flour
10 eggs
1 1/2 cups fresh lemon juice
3 tablespoons grated lemon zest
1/2 cup confectioners' sugar

These special bars were very popular at both the Utopia Bakery and Two Creek Coffeehaus. The kids at Kids Cooking Camp always love them and want to make them again every year.

Special kitchen equipment
baking parchment; stand mixer

99

Lemon Wafers

Makes 3 dozen

2¹/₂ *cups all-purpose flour*
¹/₂ *teaspoon baking powder*
¹/₂ *teaspoon salt*
³/₄ *cup (1¹/₂ sticks) unsalted butter,*
    slightly firm
1 tablespoon grated lemon zest
¹/₂ *teaspoon lemon oil*
1 cup sugar
2 eggs
¹/₂ *teaspoon vanilla extract*

This recipe was formulated for high altitude. To prepare it at low altitude, increase the baking powder to 1 teaspoon.

Special kitchen equipment
stand mixer fitted with a paddle attachment;
    baking parchment; tortilla press (optional);
    thin metal spatula

1 Sift the flour, baking powder and salt together. Combine the butter, lemon zest and lemon oil in a stand mixer fitted with a paddle attachment. Beat at medium-high speed for 1 minute or until smooth and creamy. Add the sugar gradually and beat for 2 to 3 minutes longer. Beat in the eggs one at a time. Add the vanilla and beat until smooth, scraping down the side of the bowl as needed. Add the dry ingredients in two batches, beating at low speed just until moistened.

2 Press the dough evenly in a 9×13-inch baking sheet lined with baking parchment. Cover with plastic wrap. Chill for 1 hour.

3 Shape the dough into walnut-size balls. Place one dough ball at a time between two sheets of plastic wrap in a tortilla press. Press lightly to make wafers that are thin but not too thin. Place on baking parchment-lined baking sheets and chill for 10 minutes.

4 Place the baking sheets on racks in the upper and lower thirds of a preheated 350-degree oven. Bake for 13 to 15 minutes or until the edges are light brown. Place on a wire rack and immediately loosen the wafers from the baking parchment paper with a thin metal spatula. Let stand until cool enough to handle, then remove to the wire rack to cool completely.

5 Layer the wafers between sheets of baking parchment in an airtight container and store for up to 3 weeks. Or, store cooled cookies in freezer bags in the freezer for 1 month.

Note: If the wafers do not peel off the plastic wrap easily (Step 3), they are either too warm or too thin. Reroll the dough into a ball and try again.

Cooking Under Pressure

Triple-Chocolate Cheesecake

Serves 8 to 10

Chocolate Crust
1 cup finely crushed chocolate cookies
2 tablespoons sugar
Pinch of cinnamon
2 tablespoons butter, melted

Cheesecake
16 ounces cream cheese, softened
1/3 cup sour cream or Crème Fraîche
  (page 116)
1/2 cup sugar
1/2 teaspoon instant coffee granules
1 teaspoon vanilla extract
6 ounces semisweet chocolate, melted
2 tablespoons Dutch-process baking cocoa
2 eggs, lightly beaten
1 cup water

The three layers of chocolate in this creamy cheesecake will satisfy cheesecake lovers and chocolate lovers alike. The pressure cooker cuts the cooking time from about an hour to less than 30 minutes.

Special kitchen equipment
6-inch springform pan; food processor; kitchen twine; 4- to 6-quart pressure cooker; offset spatula

Crust

1 Wrap the bottom of a buttered 6-inch springform pan with heavy-duty foil to waterproof it. Fold a long piece of foil into thirds. Place the pan on the foil to use as a cradle to lift the pan into and out of the pressure cooker.

2 Mix the cookie crumbs, sugar and cinnamon in a small bowl. Drizzle with the melted butter and mix well. Spoon into the prepared springform pan. Wrap a straight-sided flat-bottomed mug with plastic wrap and use it to press the crumb mixture evenly over the bottom and 1 inch up the side of the pan.

Cheesecake

3 Combine the cream cheese, sour cream, sugar, coffee granules and vanilla in a food processor. Pulse until mixed. Let stand to allow the coffee granules to dissolve. Add the chocolate and baking cocoa; pulse to mix well. Add the eggs and pulse just until blended; do not overmix or the cheesecake will puff too much.

4 Spoon the batter into the crust and smooth the top. Place a folded paper towel over the top of the pan and secure with double-wrapped kitchen twine. Lift the pan into the pressure cooker with the foil cradle and fold the ends of the foil to use as a lifting handle. Pour the water into the cooker to create the steam needed to cook the cheesecake.

5 Seal the lid of the cooker and place over high heat. Bring the pressure to high and cook for 15 minutes. Turn off the heat and allow the steam to dissipate completely. Remove the lid, tilting it away from you to allow the steam to escape.

6 Lift the cheesecake from the cooker using the foil cradle. Remove the twine and paper towel and loosen the cheesecake from the side of the pan with an offset spatula to keep the cheesecake from cracking.

7 Chill the cheesecake for 3 hours or longer. Place on a serving plate and remove the side of the pan. Cut with a hot knife to serve. Store, wrapped in plastic wrap, in the refrigerator for up to 5 days.

Masterful Techniques

Potato Gnocchi

Makes 130 gnocchi

2 pounds russet potatoes
2 cups all-purpose flour
1/2 cup grated Parmesan cheese
1/4 teaspoon freshly grated nutmeg
1 teaspoon kosher salt
3 egg yolks, lightly beaten
All-purpose flour for dusting
6 cups Chicken Stock (page 105) or water
Salt to taste
Olive oil for reheating
Pasta sauce of choice
Parmesan cheese, for garnish

There are basically three types of gnocchi. One is the classic Italian potato gnocchi. Another is gnocchi alla Romano, made with semolina and baked before saucing. The third is gnocchi à la Parisienne, which uses a pâte à choux dough and is poached in water. They are all delicious, but my favorite is Italian gnocchi. You can skip the step of rolling the dough pieces over a traditional gnocchi board, but the ridges help the gnocchi trap more of the sauce. This recipe will make more than is needed for a single recipe, but they freeze well and are an ideal item to have on hand.

Special kitchen equipment
potato ricer; baking parchment; gnocchi board (optional)

1 Wrap each potato in heavy-duty foil. Bake in a preheated 400-degree oven until tender. Let stand just until cool enough to handle in a kitchen towel. Peel the potatoes and cut into pieces that will fit in a potato ricer. Process the potatoes through the ricer while they are still warm for a creamier consistency. Spread evenly on a baking parchment-lined work surface and let stand until room temperature.

2 Place the potatoes in a medium-large bowl. Sprinkle with the flour, 1/2 cup Parmesan cheese, the nutmeg and 1 teaspoon kosher salt. Make a well in the center and add the egg yolks. Work the eggs into the flour with a fork. Mix the flour mixture into the potatoes, working from the outer edge to the center.

3 Knead the mixture in the bowl just until it forms a dough. Knead gently on a work surface for 4 minutes or until the dough feels dry, handling it as little as possible for light gnocchi. Cover with a dampened kitchen towel. Let rest for 30 minutes.

4 Dust a work surface with flour. Roll a small portion of the dough at a time with the palm of your hand on the work surface to form a long rope about 3/4 inch in diameter. Cut into 1/2-inch pieces with a sharp knife. Roll each piece down a gnocchi board or over the back of a kitchen fork, pressing gently to form the ridges characteristic of gnocchi.

5 Place the gnocchi in a single layer in a shallow pan dusted with flour and cover with a kitchen towel. Chill in the refrigerator for up to 6 hours or freeze for up to 1 month.

6 Bring the Stock to a rolling boil in a saucepan and season with salt to taste. Add the gnocchi and cook until the gnocchi float to the surface. Cook for 2 minutes longer or until cooked through. Remove to a bowl of cool water with a slotted spoon. Cool for 1 minute and then drain on a kitchen towel. Spread on a baking sheet lined with baking parchment. Store in the refrigerator for use within 24 hours or freeze for several weeks in freezer bags.

7 To reheat the gnocchi, heat a small amount of olive oil in a large sauté pan over medium heat until it begins to shimmer. Pour off any excess oil, leaving just enough to coat the pan. Add the gnocchi and cook for 1 to 2 minutes or until golden brown on the bottom. Serve by folding gently into the desired pasta sauce and spooning into warm bowls; garnish with additional Parmesan cheese.

Red Curry Paste

1 Combine the red chiles with enough warm water to cover in a bowl; let stand to soak. Wrap the shrimp paste in foil. Place over a low flame and heat on both sides for 30 seconds or until toasted.

2 Combine the coriander seeds, cumin seeds and white peppercorns in a dry sauté pan. Toast just until smoky. Cool and then place in a mortar and crush with a pestle. Drain the chiles and add to the mortar with the shrimp paste, lemon grass, galangal, lime zest and cilantro root; pound into a smooth paste. Add the garlic, shallots, Thai chiles and kosher salt and pound to form a smooth deep red paste.

Note: To prepare this in a small food processor, add up to 3 tablespoons water to facilitate blending. Start with the wet ingredients, such as shallots, garlic and fresh chiles, and add the dry ingredients later, pulsing to mix and scraping the side of the food processor frequently.

Makes 1 cup

14 dried long red chiles, seeds removed
1 teaspoon Thai shrimp paste
2 teaspoons coriander seeds
1 teaspoon cumin seeds
1/2 teaspoon white peppercorns
3 stalks lemon grass, tender inner portions only, thinly sliced
1 tablespoon grated galangal (Thai ginger)
1 teaspoon grated lime zest
2 teaspoons chopped cilantro root or stems
5 garlic cloves, crushed
2 shallots, sliced
4 Thai bird chiles
2 teaspoons kosher salt

The zest of kaffir limes works best in this paste, but if they are not available, you can instead add kaffir lime leaves to the curry you make from it. Paprika enhances the brilliant red of the paste, and dried chilies spice it up. Use 1 tablespoon crushed red pepper in place of the dried chiles if you prefer a milder flavor.

Special kitchen equipment
mortar and pestle or small food processor

113

Roasted Garlic

Makes about ¹/₄ cup

1 whole garlic bulb
2 tablespoons olive oil

1 Cut the top from the garlic bulb to expose the ends of the cloves and place the bulb in the center of a square of foil. Drizzle with the olive oil, coating the tops of the cloves well. Pull up the edges of the foil to enclose the bulb completely.

2 Place in a baking dish and bake in a preheated 350-degree oven for 30 to 35 minutes or until tender. Cool to room temperature in the foil packet. Press the cloves to remove them from the skins.

Pasta Fresca

Makes 6 servings

2¹/₂ cups (or more) all-purpose flour
2 teaspoons kosher salt
4 eggs
2 tablespoons olive oil

Fresh pasta cooks much faster that dried pasta. To cook it, bring water to a boil in a saucepan over high heat and add ¹/₂ tablespoon salt. Add the pasta to the water as soon as it begins to boil and use a pasta rake or large fork to separate the strands and ensure even cooking. Test for doneness after one minute, remembering that it will continue to cook until it is drained.

Special kitchen equipment
food processor; stand mixer fitted with a flat roller pasta attachment and a cutter attachment

1 Combine the flour and kosher salt in a food processor and pulse two or three times to mix. Add the eggs and olive oil and pulse just until the flour is moistened and the mixture begins to form a ball. Add 1 or 2 tablespoons additional flour if needed to form a ball, processing constantly until the ball turns around the bowl about twenty times.

2 Knead the dough on a lightly floured work surface to form a smooth ball. Place a bowl upside down on the dough and let rest for 30 minutes. Cut the dough into four portions and cover three of the portions with plastic wrap.

3 Set the flat roller pasta attachment of a stand mixer at the widest setting and roll one portion of the dough through it. Fold the dough two or three times and run it through the machine five to seven times at the wide setting or until it is satin smooth and elastic, dusting it with flour if it becomes too sticky; the dough should be stiff but not tough.

4 Continue to run the dough through the machine at increasingly narrow settings until it is the thickness of a file folder at the thinnest setting. Repeat the process with the remaining dough.

5 Replace the roller attachment with a cutter attachment. Flour the dough lightly and run it through the machine to cut as desired. Cook immediately or store in a sealable plastic bag in the refrigerator for up to 24 hours.

Masterful Techniques

115

Crème Fraîche

Makes about 1 cup

1 cup heavy cream
2 tablespoons buttermilk

Combine the cream and buttermilk in a glass bowl or jar. Let stand, uncovered, at a room temperature of about 70 degrees for 8 to 24 hours or until very thick; stir well. Store, covered, in the refrigerator for up to 10 days. Serve over fresh fruit or warm desserts, such as cobblers or pudding.

Note: The matured, thickened cream has a slightly tangy, nutty flavor and a velvety rich texture. The thickness can range from that of commercial sour cream to almost solid. In the United States, where all commercial cream is pasteurized, the agents necessary for fermenting crème fraîche can be buttermilk or sour cream. An expensive version of it can be purchased in supermarkets, but it is easy to make this equally delicious version at home

Herb Crème Fraîche

Makes 3/4 cup

3/4 cup Crème Fraîche (above)
16 chives, coarsely chopped
2 tablespoons dill weed
Kosher salt to taste

Combine the Crème Fraîche, chives and dill weed in a medium bowl. Process with an immersion blender until smooth and season with kosher salt.

Balsamic Reduction

Makes about 1 cup

2 cups balsamic vinegar

Bring the balsamic vinegar to a boil in a small nonreactive saucepan over medium heat. Reduce the heat to a simmer and simmer until the mixture is thick enough to coat the back of a spoon. Cool to room temperature.

Mayonnaise

Makes 1 1/2 cups

2 egg yolks
1 tablespoon Dijon mustard
1 teaspoon fresh lemon juice or
*   wine vinegar*
2 tablespoons chopped fresh herbs,
*   or 2 garlic cloves (optional)*
Salt and pepper to taste
1 cup olive oil

Special kitchen equipment
blender or food processor

Process the egg yolks in a blender or food processor until pale yellow and thick. Add the Dijon mustard, lemon juice and herbs. Season with salt and pepper and process for 1 minute. Add the olive oil gradually in a steady stream, processing constantly until the mixture has thickened and emulsified. Thin with a few drops of water or additional lemon juice if the mayonnaise appears too thick. Store, tightly covered, in the refrigerator for up to 3 days.

Note: If you are concerned about using raw egg yolks, use egg yolks pasteurized in their shells or use an equivalent amount of pasteurized egg substitute.

Clarified Butter

Makes about 1 1/2 cups

2 cups (4 sticks) unsalted butter

1 Place the butter in a microwave-safe bowl large enough to hold it when melted. Microwave at Medium for 30 seconds; microwave at 20-second intervals until the butter is completely melted.

2 Place the bowl on a flat surface and let stand until all the milk solids sink to the bottom of the bowl. Chill in the refrigerator until firm.

3 Loosen the butter from the bowl with the tip of a knife. Invert the solid butter onto a plate, and discard the liquid. Cut the butter into 2-tablespoon pieces and place in an sealable plastic bag. Store in the refrigerator.

Clarified butter is also known as drawn butter. It is unsalted butter that has melted slowly, allowing most of the water to evaporate and the solids to sink to the bottom of the bowl. I usually clarify one pound of butter, to have it on hand, but you can clarify a smaller amount if you prefer.

Classic Puff Pastry (Pâte Feuilletée)

Makes 2 1/2 pounds

1 1/2 teaspoons salt
1/4 cup water
3 1/4 cups all-purpose flour
3 tablespoons unsalted butter,
 slightly softened
3/4 cup water
2 cups (4 sticks) unsalted butter,
 slightly softened
3/4 cup all-purpose flour
Additional flour for sprinkling

To bake puff pastry, cut the pastry into the desired shapes and then chill. Brush with an egg wash, taking care not to brush the edges, which would seal them and inhibit rising. Bake in a preheated 450-degree oven until the pastry begins to brown. Reduce the temperature to 375 degrees and prop the oven open with the handle of a long wooden spoon to release the moisture from the oven. Bake until the tops are dark golden brown and the pastry is cooked through. To add a sweet glaze, sift confectioners' sugar over the top and broil just until it caramelizes. Cool completely on a wire rack before filling and serving.

Special kitchen equipment
stand mixer fitted with a
 paddle attachment

1 Combine the salt and 1/4 cup water in a stand mixer fitted with a paddle attachment and mix to dissolve the salt. Add 3 1/4 cups flour and 3 tablespoons butter, beating at low speed until the butter is completely incorporated. Add 3/4 cup water and beat until the mixture comes together to form a dough. Add additional water one tablespoon at a time if needed to form a firm but not hard dough.

2 Shape the dough into a ball on a lightly floured work surface; flatten slightly. Cut an "X" 1/4 inch deep in the top of the ball with a sharp knife to release the elasticity. Wrap with plastic wrap and let stand in the refrigerator for 2 hours or longer.

3 Place 2 cups butter in the mixer fitted with the paddle attachment and beat until softened. Add 3/4 cup flour and mix well. Shape into a ball and place on a sheet of plastic wrap sprinkled with flour. Sprinkle about 1 tablespoon flour over the ball and fold the plastic wrap over the top.

4 Roll the butter mixture into a 6×6-inch square; the mixture should not crack or crumble around the edges. Cover loosely with plastic wrap. Chill for 30 minutes if the butter mixture becomes sticky or begins to melt. Place the plastic-wrapped square on a baking sheet and chill for 2 hours or until firm but not hard.

5 Scrape the work surface clean and sprinkle lightly with flour. Roll the chilled dough into a 10×10-inch square. Place the butter square on the dough at a 45-degree angle. Fold in the corners of the dough square to meet in the center of the butter square; pinch the seams to seal.

6 Sprinkle the dough lightly with flour and roll to a 10×22-inch rectangle. Fold the rectangle crosswise into thirds; this is referred to as a single turn and will consist of three layers of dough. Return to the baking sheet and chill, covered with plastic wrap, for 30 minutes.

7 Roll the dough into a 10×22-inch rectangle again on a lightly floured surface. Fold the dough crosswise into halves and then into halves again; this is called a double turn and will consist of four layers. Chill for 30 minutes longer.

8 Repeat the processes for another single turn and another double turn, chilling after each procedure. Wrap in plastic wrap and chill for 2 hours or up to 1 week before using.

Lemon Curd

Makes 2 cups

8 egg yolks
1 1/3 cups sugar
3/4 cup fresh lemon juice (6 to 8 lemons)
1/2 cup (1 stick) unsalted butter
1/4 cup grated lemon zest, grated with
  a microplane

had an unusual cooking experience a while back. For lemon curd, I used fresh farm eggs that had only been gathered one or two days before and found that the curd thickened in less than half the time.

Special kitchen equipment
microplane zester; thermometer; strainer

1 Combine the egg yolks, sugar and lemon juice in a medium saucepan. Add the butter. Cook over low heat for 20 minutes, maintaining the temperature between 135 and 145 degrees on a thermometer, stirring frequently. Cook for 10 to 20 minutes longer or until thick enough to coat the back of the spoon, allowing the temperature to rise no higher than 170 degrees and stirring frequently; do not boil.

2 Pour through a strainer into a glass bowl. Stir in the zest and place plastic wrap directly on the surface to keep a skin from forming. Chill for 2 hours or up to 2 weeks.

Note: This is the classic English lemon curd famous as an accompaniment for scones. In the United States, we have found many more uses for lemon curd. You can substitute lime juice and zest or grapefruit juice and zest to vary the flavor.

Cranberry Fruit Compote

Makes 4 cups

12 ounces fresh cranberries
1 3/4 cups sugar
1 cup water
1 Granny Smith apple, peeled,
    cored and chopped
Juice and grated zest of 1 orange
Juice and grated zest of 1 lemon
3/4 cup golden raisinis
3/4 cup walnuts, toasted
    and chopped

1 Combine the cranberries, sugar and water in a medium saucepan. Cook over low heat for 5 minutes or until the cranberry skins pop. Add the apple, orange juice, orange zest, lemon juice and lemon zest. Cook for 15 minutes longer.

2 Remove from the heat and stir in the raisins and walnuts. Let stand until cool. Store in the refrigerator for up to 2 weeks.

Note: The compote is good with any poultry, especially roast turkey. It's a great wintertime addition to turkey sandwiches. I love to use it as a filling for Brie en Croûte (page 22).

You can soak the raisins in brandy or rum if desired.

Easy Dark Chocolate Filling

Makes 3 cups

2 cups heavy cream
7 ounces bittersweet chocolate,
    finely chopped
1 teaspoon vanilla extract, or
    1 tablespoon Cognac, Grand
    Marnier, Kahlúa or other liqueur

1 Bring the cream to a gentle boil in a medium saucepan over medium-high heat. Pour over the chocolate in a heatproof bowl and let stand for 1 minute to melt the chocolate. Whisk until smooth. Whisk in the vanilla. Place plastic wrap directly on the surface. Let stand until room temperature. Chill for 6 hours or until firm enough to whip.

2 Beat at high speed in a stand mixer fitted with a whisk attachment for 1 minute or just until the mixture forms soft peaks and is firm enough to spread; do not overbeat. Use immediately or store in an airtight container in the refrigerator for up to 1 week. Bring to room temperature before using.

Finely ground nuts are a nice addition to this filling.

Special kitchen equipment
stand mixer fitted with a whisk
    attachment

Limoncello

Makes 6 cups

6 organic lemons
3 cups (100-proof) unflavored vodka
3 cups spring water
1 1/2 cups sugar

Limoncello is a popular Italian liqueur. It is best served chilled and sipped slowly. Limoncello makes a nice gift for a friend. It is important to use organic lemons for this recipe because they have no wax coating.

Special kitchen equipment
sharp vegetable peeler; strainer

1 Wash and dry the lemons. Remove just the yellow zest in thin strips with a sharp vegetable peeler, leaving the bitter white pith. Reserve the lemons for another use. Combine the zest with the vodka in a half-gallon jar with a tight-fitting lid. Seal and place in a dark place. Let stand at room temperature for 1 to 3 months, or until the lemon peels are pale yellow and the vodka is deep yellow.

2 Pour through a strainer into a glass container; reserve the vodka. Place the strainer with the lemon zest over a heatproof glass bowl.

3 Combine the water and sugar in a saucepan and bring to a boil, stirring to dissolve the sugar completely. Boil for 3 minutes. Pour over the lemon zest into the heatproof bowl, pressing on the zest to extract as much liquid as possible. Discard the zest and allow the liquid to cool.

4 Add the cooled liquid to the lemon-infused vodka and mix well. Pour into bottles and seal tightly. Let stand for 5 days or longer. Store in the freezer indefinitely.

Mail-Order Sources

The Baker's Catalogue
800-827-6836

Kitchen Krafts
800-776-0575

Brix of Napa Valley
877-944-2749

Napa Style
866-944-2749

Chef's Catalogue
800-338-3232

Wine Enthusiast
800-356-8466

Kelley's Katch Caviar
731-925-7360

Local Sources

Anaya's Market (Mexican)
1490 Munchkin Road
Park City, Utah 84060
435-615-8454

Southeast Supermarket
422 East 900 South
Salt Lake City, Utah 84111
801-363-5474

Emigration Market
featuring USDA Choice Meats
1796 East 1300 South
Salt Lake City, Utah 84108

Spoons 'n Spice
4700 South 900 East #45
Salt Lake City, Utah 84117
801-263-1898

Gygi Culinary Solutions
3500 South 300 West
Salt Lake City, Utah 84115
801-268-3316

Sur la Table
The Gateway Mall
Salt Lake City, Utah 84101
801-456-0280

La Niche Gourmet and Gifts
401 Main Street
Park City, Utah 84060
435-649-2372

Williams-Sonoma
Trolley Square Shopping Mall
Salt Lake City, Utah 84102

Liberty Heights Fresh
1300 South at 1100 East
Salt Lake City, Utah 84152
801-58FRESH

Index

Additional copies of

Cooking with
Jaxon

are available by visiting
www.parkcitycookingschool.com and
clicking "cookbook."